PROCLAMATION COMMENTARIES

The New Testament Witnesses for Preaching   Gerhard Krodel, *Editor*

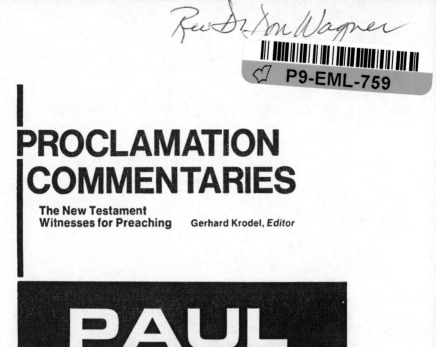

PAUL
AND HIS LETTERS

Leander E. Keck

FORTRESS PRESS   Philadelphia, Pennsylvania

To
Ernst Käsemann
with gratitude

Fourth printing 1982

Library of Congress Cataloging in Publication Data
Keck, Leander E
    Paul and his letters.

    (Proclamation commentaries: The New Testament witnesses for preaching)
    Bibliography: p.
    Includes index.
    1. Bible. N.T. Epistles of Paul—Theology.
2. Paul, Saint, Apostle. I. Title.
BS2651.K42   227'.06   78-54554
ISBN 0-8006-0587-X

9962K82   Printed in the United States of America   1-587

CONTENTS

EDITOR'S FOREWORD

With a directness that was typical of him, Paul claimed, "I have worked harder than any" of the other apostles (1 Cor. 15:10). Concerning the geography of his "harder" work, he asserted: "From Jerusalem as far round as Illyricum I have fully preached the gospel of Christ . . . and now since I no longer have any room for work in these regions . . . I hope to see you in passing as I go to Spain" (Rom. 15:19, 23, 24). In terms of hardship he could boast that his life included "countless beatings and often near death" (2 Cor. 11:23-27; 6:4-5; 4:8-10). At the end there awaited martyrdom as the reward for his labors and the fitting conclusion of the work of one who had carried on his body "the marks of Jesus" as badges of honor (Gal. 6:17). During his apostleship he felt "the daily pressure . . . for all the churches" (2 Cor. 11:28) and worried about his newly established communities. The tone of his letters varied greatly. He could threaten his small house churches: "Shall I come to you with a rod?" (1 Cor. 4:21); be sarcastic (Gal. 5:12); emotional (Gal. 4:12-20); he could exhort them "like a father with his children" (1 Thess. 2:11); or remind them that he is "gentle like a nurse" (1 Thess. 2:7). The apostle who wanted to be "all things to all men" (1 Cor. 9:22) urged his children to "be imitators of me" (1 Cor. 4:16; 10:33) as they learned to live by faith in Christ crucified and resurrected.

To Paul's claim to have been the most hard-working apostle, we can add that he was the only apostle to leave us a written legacy. Moreover, his letters are the earliest writings of the NT. The other writings of the NT are either anonymous or pseudonymous and reflect apostolic teaching only indirectly. Even Paul's opponents admit "his letters are weighty and strong in contrast to his physical appearance (hē parousia tou sōmatos) which is weak and his speaking ability which is awful" (2 Cor. 10:10).

Through his letters the tireless missionary apostle reveals himself to be the foremost first century theologian who creatively adopted and adapted the traditions of his church, and who, in his letters, interpreted the one gospel in diverse situations of crisis in which his churches found themselves. Though Paul the theologian is always difficult to understand—2 Pet. 3:15 already took note of this—and frequently he is misunderstood by friend and foe alike, nevertheless, his influence extended across the centuries. Like no other theologian before or after, he became the occasion and source for the revitalization of Christianity through theologians such as Augustine, Luther, and Barth, while simultaneously he informed the theological reflection and piety of countless women and men, clergy and laypersons. It is always worthwhile to rediscover Paul, even if our discovery of his message and his theology is only "in part," like all *gnosis* (1 Cor. 13:12).

This volume is a creative rediscovery of Paul. Influenced by Ernst Käsemann whose commentary on Romans represents a milestone in Pauline interpretation, Leander Keck first presents problems surrounding Paul. In the second part he deals with the common ground between Paul and the recipients of his letters. Keck locates the center of Paul's gospel in the cross and the resurrection and the salvific response to it. The high point of this part is found in the chapter on the deeper logic of the gospel. Here the author masterfully deals with God's sovereign freedom from the perspectives of 1) intentionality and achievement and 2) newness and constancy. He then continues to probe the dimensions of creation and new creation with a presentation of the Christian participation in Christ and anticipation of the eschaton as the horizon of participation in Christ. Lastly Keck deals with three theological positions Paul hammered out in the heat of controversy—sola fide, the Spirit as the power sphere of the new age, and justification. Simultaneously he draws brief, precise lines of demarcation to alternate interpretations of Paul by Stendahl and Sanders.

Leander Keck is Dean and Winkley Professor of Biblical Theology at Yale Divinity School. He is the editor of the Lives of Jesus Series, coeditor of *Studies in Luke-Acts,* and author of numerous articles and books.

Lutheran Theological Seminary at Gettysburg   GERHARD KRODEL

INTRODUCTION

Paul deserves to be discovered by those who do not know his letters and to be discovered afresh by those who do. He is not always easy to understand, and often difficult to accept. Still, again and again readers have found him to have a word for the times.

No one can prescribe how Paul is to be discovered, or predict which facets of his thought will be most pertinent. One can, however, provide some help by making him more accessible, by sketching his message as a whole.

Paul's letters addressed particular issues in small house churches. Reading these letters is somewhat like overhearing a telephone conversation: one must always infer what is being said at the other end of the line, as well as the context of the conversation. Every critical introduction to the NT therefore places the individual letters into an inferred context. That sort of information will not be repeated. What interests us here is its import for our understanding of Paul and his letters as a whole.

The man and his message are not identical with the letters. Accordingly, the present volume is divided into three parts. Part One ("The Quest for the Historical Paul") takes note of major issues which have emerged in Pauline studies. Part Two ("The Gospel Paul Preached") attempts to discern Paul's message apart from the controversies which evoked the letters. Paul was the bearer and interpreter of certain traditions, a particular form of early Christianity. Because most of his original readers had heard him before they read his letters, both he and they could assume a great deal in their conversation. Getting a sense of this common ground is the aim of Part Two. "What Paul Fought For" (Part Three) deals with fundamental themes which Paul asserted and defended in the letters. Naturally, the distinction between Part Two and Part Three is not exact. Even so, it situates Paul's theology between his background in early Christianity and his foreground in the crises of his churches. That is where the Paul we know theologized.

The letters of Paul are events in which Christian traditions were being interpreted into the lives and thoughts of real people. Today, Paul himself has become part of the Christian tradition. Nonetheless, he has the capacity to interact also with today's readers, who may be as surprised by him as those who read his letters first. That is what discovering Paul is all about. Even those who "know Paul" can discover him afresh.

PART I

THE QUEST FOR THE HISTORICAL PAUL

CHAPTER ONE

PAUL THE PROBLEM

Probably no other Christian has been hated so intensely as Paul. Even those who do not despise him may regret his influence on Christianity in the first place. They hold him responsible for displacing the religion of Jesus himself with a religion about Jesus, one represented by a church which preaches Jesus as a divine savior from sin, administers sacraments, and ordains clergy—none of which Jesus had inaugurated. A second group are the Jews. They blame Paul, the great apostate, for the fact that Christians have a distorted view of Judaism. Only recently have a few Jewish scholars found it possible to write appreciatively about Paul, while dissenting from him. Those women who blame Paul for their second-class status in the church, and their inferior role in a culture shaped by it, are a third group alienated from Paul. To some extent, all three groups have misunderstood him; perhaps seeing him in his historical context will alleviate some of the animus. But it is important to acknowledge at the outset that Paul is far from everybody's favorite Christian.

For those who admire Paul, he may be more of a problem than they realize. Can one be a sound representative of the gospel and seldom quote Jesus? How valid an interpreter of Christianity is Paul? The more apparent it becomes that Paul's theology is not interchangeable with that of John, for instance, the clearer it is that Paul does not speak for the whole NT. Indeed, does he speak for anyone but himself? If one stands with Paul, does one stand with a loner, with one who could write that there is no valid gospel other than his, even if an angel were to preach it (Gal. 1:8)? Does an adequate view of Christianity require us to supplement Paul,

2

to round off his sharp edges and to domesticate him into the mainstream? Many have thought so.

Seeing Paul historically will not solve all problems readers have had with him, or might discover in him, but it is one way of getting some perspective. Consequently, this chapter will sketch three historical aspects of the problem of Paul.

THE PROBLEM OF PAUL IN THE NEW TESTAMENT

First, Paul presents a problem within the NT because he dominates it. Of the 657 pages of Greek text (Nestle edition), 156 claim to come from Paul. If we add the 24 pages of the Letter to the Hebrews, which got into the canon because the church in Egypt believed Paul wrote it, more than one fourth of the NT is associated with a man who had not been a disciple of Jesus, whereas Peter, the leading figure in the circle around Jesus, is represented by only 14 pages. In addition, more than half of the Book of Acts is devoted to Paul. Did Paul dominate Christianity in his own time as much as he now dominates the NT? Or does Paul's place in the canon make him loom larger than he actually was? Second, Paul appears as a problem in the NT because the letters from the man often do not support the report about him in Acts. Because the Paul of Acts is the Paul most people know best, one should guard against assimilating the Paul of the Letters to the Paul of Acts. The Paul of the Letters must determine our understanding of the man. Acts is a secondary source for historical inquiry; the first hand sources are the letters. Nonetheless, Acts remains the only account of Paul's career that we have from the first centuries, and no study of Paul can ignore it completely. (See *Acts:* forthcoming volume in *Proclamation Commentaries* series.)

The letters themselves constitute the third way in which Paul is a problem in the NT, for there are such fundamental differences among them that most scholars are convinced that some cannot have come from Paul.

There is virtual unanimity that the following letters are authentic: Romans, 1, 2 Corinthians, Galatians, Philippians, 1 Thessalonians, Philemon; there is almost equal agreement that the Pastorals (1, 2 Timothy, Titus) are not genuine. The majority of students regard Ephesians to be non-genuine as well, but opinion is divided over Colossians and 2 Thessalonians.

For our purposes, it is more important to see the consequences of regarding only the seven letters as genuine than it is to justify not expanding the list. First of all, if the seven letters are genuine, any interpretation of Paul which restricts itself to them rests on a solid base; the more one relies on what is said only in Ephesians or 2 Thessalonians, for instance, the less secure is the interpretation of Paul. In no case should a disputed letter be the basis for interpreting something in a genuine letter. For example, Col. 3:1 speaks of the believer as already having been raised with Christ; this must not guide the interpretation of Rom. 6:5, where Paul writes that participation in Christ's resurrection is a future event.

Moreover, the distinctive emphasis of each deutero-Pauline letter is so pronounced that including them in a discussion of Paul himself shifts the center of gravity. This is especially true of Ephesians, in which the church is the central theme. Not surprisingly, those interpretations of Paul which emphasize his ecclesiology rely on Ephesians, and read the theology of the genuine letters through the lens of this deutero-Pauline one.

Further, if it is indeed the case, as I think likely, that Philippians and Philemon were written from Ephesus, then all seven letters were written in the 50s. This chronological conclusion has important implications. (a) The earliest letter is 1 Thessalonians and Romans is the latest. Behind Romans, the most mature statement of Paul's theology, lie the controversies worked through in previous letter-writing. (b) The closer the letters stand to one another in time, the less persuasive are efforts to trace development in Paul's thought. Differences within the genuine letters must be accounted for on a basis other than development in Paul's thinking. (c) Our letters come from but a slice of Paul's career. From the fifteen years between his conversion and 1 Thessalonians we have nothing except reports in Acts; likewise we have nothing from the last decade when he was a prisoner in Palestine and in Rome except reports in Acts.

Finally, the consequences we have noted are all historical, not theological. That is, they concern attempts to understand Paul himself in his own context, not with the theological validity of the deutero-Pauline letters, nor with their authority in the canon. What Ephesians says about the church may or may not be valid, irrespective of whether or not Paul wrote it. The interpreter of the NT needs to be clear on this point, lest historical conclusions and hypotheses prejudge theological issues improperly.

To conclude, "the message of Paul" is not self-evident because there are different "Pauls" in the NT. Indeed, the latest book in the NT points out that the church was having trouble understanding him properly (2 Pet. 3:15-16). Also in the ancient church Paul was a problem.

PAUL THE PROBLEM IN EARLY CHRISTIANITY

To understand better Paul's place in early Christianity, it is necessary to see that the NT itself incorporates alternative interpretations of the gospel. Paul does not speak for everyone. It is useful to recognize several of the types of Christianity which were developing in the first century.

To begin with, the Christianity which developed in Jerusalem differed markedly from Paul's. The modern study of Paul began in the 1830s when F. C. Baur contended that the whole apostolic period was dominated by a tension between Jewish Christianity led by Peter and a gentile Christianity represented by Paul. In one way or other, this theory has persisted, even though today it is not Peter but James, Jesus' brother, who is credited with leading a Christianized Judaism in Jerusalem. James' Christianity (not to be associated with the Epistle of James, written by someone else) insisted on observing the Jewish law (Acts 21:18-20). We see this also in the tradition quoted by the fourth century historian, Eusebius, concerning James: he was a very devout Jew, praying so often in the temple that he got calluses on his knees like a camel. Baur and his successors may have exaggerated certain aspects of the tension between Paul and James, and Johannes Munck (*Paul and the Salvation of Mankind*) may have underestimated it, but there is no doubt that the differences were deep.

Another type of Christianity differed from that of both James and Paul, namely, the Johannine. Deissmann (*Paul,* p. 7)was wrong in calling John Paul's greatest interpreter, for John does not develop Pauline Christianity but represents another alternative to it. Bultmann (*Theology of the New Testament* 2, pp. 7–10) rightly saw that themes important to Paul are absent from John (e.g., the problem of the law). Besides, what is important to John is not found in Paul (e.g., the Paraclete).

There was also outright opposition to Paul, both in his own time and afterward. As we shall see, Paul had to contend with the opposition even in his own churches, especially in Galatia and Corinth. Traveling preachers appeared in Corinth after he had left and undermined his work there so seriously that he said they were "false apostles, deceitful workmen, disguising themselves as apostles of Christ" (2 Cor. 11:13). Similarly, he was so irritated at those who opposed his gospel in Galatia by demanding that gentile Christians circumcise themselves, that he wished the knife would slip during the operation (Gal. 5:12). Long afterward, in the second century, the Ebionites (Jewish Christians who called themselves "the Poor" and claimed to be the descendants from the original church) hated Paul as the arch-heretic.

Finally, the friends of Paul struggled not only against his enemies but to some extent also with each other for the rights to Paul's legacy (as 2 Peter saw). Acts aims to present a normative account of Paul, portraying him as acknowledged by the Jerusalem church. This insistence that Paul was in good standing with the Jerusalem church shows that it was necessary to defend Paul and his successors from the charge of being "Paulinists"— a sectarian movement. Moreover, Acts shows Paul to be as loyal a Jew as he could have been under the circumstances. He circumcised Timothy even though it was not necessary theologically (Acts 16:1–3); Paul was eager to observe the Jewish festival of Pentecost in Jerusalem, like a pilgrim (Acts 20:16). Once there, he agreed to James's strategy for showing that he was faithful to Judaism (Acts 21:17–26). Before the Sanhedrin, Acts has Paul claim he is (not "was") a Pharisee, whose advocacy of the resurrection doctrine succeeded in dividing the court (Acts 23:1–10). Apparently Acts is defending Paul, and thereby the Christians who look to him, from the charge of being a renegade Jew. This may well have been a problem in Luke's generation, which needed to know who Paul really was.

Some friends of Paul also produced letters in his name and each document pulls Paul in a different direction. Ephesians emphasizes ecclesiology; the Pastorals present him as the advocate of a highly institutionalized church. On the other hand, 2 Thessalonians makes Paul combat another (now lost) spurious letter circulating in his name (2 Thess. 2:2), and has him advocate an outright apocalyptic teaching. The spurious letter attacked by 2 Thessalonians advocated a position similar to that opposed by 2 Timothy—that the Day of the Lord had already come (2 Tim. 2:16-18). This is the sign of a gnostic interpretation of Paul. Recently, Elaine Pagels analyzed the ways second century Valentinian gnostics interpreted Paul along Valentinian lines (*The Gnostic Paul*). Later still, the apocryphal correspondence between Paul and Seneca portrayed Paul in somewhat Stoicized terms. Still later, the Acts of Paul had him advocate Christian asceticism.

The most ardent friend of Paul in the early second century was Marcion, who concluded that after Paul's death his Judaizing opponents not only prevailed and Judaized Christianity but tampered with his letters in order to make Paul speak favorably of the OT and of the Creator. In the name of Paul, Marcion became the first reformer, and he split many churches. He decided that Paul's gospel had been the Gospel of Luke (also corrupted by the Judaizers). To restore true Christianity, he purged the letters of Paul and the Gospel of Luke of the pro-OT parts and so provided his churches with the first distinctly Christian canon—the Gospel of Luke and the Letters of Paul (minus the Pastorals). A major achievement of Irenaeus and Tertullian was to reclaim Paul from some of his most ardent friends, the gnostics and Marcion, by showing that Paul's real friends were in the emerging catholic church. The catholicity of the church manifests itself in the fact that the NT includes epistles attributed to apostles besides Paul (Peter, John, James, Jude), and Gospels besides Luke.

Enough of this fascinating story has been sketched to show that Paul was a controversial figure in early Christianity. The Christians of the early centuries too wrestled with the problem, Who was Paul really and what did he really teach? In modern times, the controversies have resumed.

THE PROBLEM OF PAUL IN CRITICAL SCHOLARSHIP

Modern students of Paul are perplexed by certain aspects of his life and thought, especially the dominant cultural-religious influence upon him. Is he to be understood primarily in light of Hellenistic religiosity or in light of Judaism? Or are these false alternatives?

Attempts to understand Paul primarily in terms of Hellenism tend to emphasize either his view of the sacraments or his Christology. The former calls attention to the theme of participating in Christ's death through baptism and the Lord's Supper, the latter to his view of Christ as the divine being who descended to earth where he achieved salvation and then was exalted to God's right hand.

Paul's view of the sacraments has sometimes been seen to reflect those Hellenistic mystery cults in which the initiate appropriated the divine life/death of the deity, and so was reborn. According to this view, the almost "magical" power of baptism manifests itself in the casual way in which Paul mentions the baptism for the dead (1 Cor. 15:29). So potent is the sacramental eating of the Lord's body that those who ate "unworthily" became ill and some died (1 Cor. 11:29–30). Such passages, often bypassed by readers, are said to be tips of the icebergs, revealing that Paul owes far more to the mystery cults than appears on the surface. Since there is no Jewish precedent for such ideas as participating in the deity's death (Rom. 6:5), it must be from the cults that Paul derived them.

However, there are formidable obstacles to reading Paul in this light. For one thing, he never uses the term "rebirth" nor does he appear to have made baptismal initiation central to his work (1 Cor. 1:14–17, see chapter 4). Moreover, the reference to baptism for the dead is too obscure to become the basis of interpretation. Above all, although the cults were ancient already in Paul's time, it is not clear that they were a major factor on the scene in his day. Rather they seem to have become more prominent only later. The attempts to interpret Paul in light of the mystery cults did, however, call attention to the "realism" of Paul's language about participation in Christ's death and signaled the need to be wary of taking such language to be "merely symbolic"—a way of talking that neither Paul nor anyone else in his time would have understood.

The Hellenistic interpretation of Paul has emphasized also his indebtedness to the myth of the descending/ascending redeemer, especially as this has been found in Gnosticism. Sometimes this is connected with the myth of the Primal Man, Anthropos, which has been traced far back into antiquity. 1 Cor. 15:45–49 speaks of the "man from heaven" who is to embody human destiny in contrast with Adam, the "man of dust" who constitutes human fate. Sometimes this myth of the redeemer, who himself was redeemed from human existence which he assumed, is found behind Phil. 2:5–11, which celebrates the humiliation/exaltation of God's Son, or behind 1 Cor. 2:8 which speaks of the incognito appearing of the Son on earth, who has slipped by the invisible powers which dominate the globe (see chapter 5). This myth is intimately bound up with the gnostic view of redemption, which will concern us in chapter 7. It is also linked with the idea that the saved constitute a "body" whose "head" is the redeemer—a view found in Col. 1:18 and Eph. 4:15–16, and which may lie behind 1 Cor. 12:27 (which does not mention the "head"). Moreover, in 1 Corinthians 2–3 Paul appears to reason like a gnostic who claims that as a Spirit-person, he can know what no one else can know.

Many students have serious problems with any interpretation of Paul which relies on texts later than Paul to reconstruct backgrounds that influenced him. This is the case for the alleged gnostic influence on Paul's Christology. This objection can be easily overemphasized and made into a false refuge, because the later texts (the only ones available) clearly contain ideas which were much older and which do illumine Paul's assertions. More important, it has been shown that the redeemed redeemer myth is largely a composite made by modern scholars who drew a variety of material together, and that in Paul's day there was no single dominant redeemer myth. Nonetheless, the many myths do fall into a certain pattern, and the pattern was probably taken for granted by Paul and his readers. In other words, there is more reason to associate Paul's Christology with Hellenistic mythology than there is to derive his view of the sacraments from mystery cults.

Attempts to understand Paul primarily in terms of Judaism tend to emphasize one of three types of Judaism: Hellenistic, rabbinic, or apocalyptic. That Paul was a Hellenized Jew is evident not only by his mastery of the Septuagint (the translation of the synagogue Bible into Greek, made several centuries before), but also by his competent use of Greek rhetorical forms (see chapter 2). Furthermore, in 1 Cor. 1:24 he calls Christ the wisdom of God, a standard motif of Hellenized Judaism. Likewise, Rom. 1:18-32 echoes Hellenistic Jewish attitudes toward gentiles.

That Paul was trained in Pharisaic Judaism in Jerusalem is reported in Acts 22:3. Moreover, although Paul himself never refers to his studying with Gamaliel in Jerusalem, he does refer to his pre-Christian life as a Pharisee (Phil. 3:4-5) and to his previous zeal for the traditions of his fathers (Gal. 1:14). He not only uses the technical rabbinic vocabulary for receiving and transmitting traditions (1 Cor. 15:3) but also argues from Scripture in rabbinic ways and relies on traditions developed among the rabbis (1 Cor. 10:1-5). Above all, Paul's concern to relate Christ to the law of Moses—the central theme of Pharisaism—manifests the abiding influence of this aspect of Judaism upon him. As we shall see, it is *what* Paul says about the law which causes some scholars to conclude that he misrepresented Pharisaism.

Paul also appears to have been deeply affected by another strand of Judaism—apocalyptic. Unless apocalyptic Jewish ideas reached Paul through the Christian community, one must assume that Paul had been influenced by Jewish apocalyptic before he became a Christian. Again, what Paul appears to assume suggests the deep influence of apocalyptic upon him—ideas like the wrath of God (Rom. 1:18), the coming judgment (1 Cor. 4:4-5), the notion that God sets the times (Gal. 4:4), the suddenness of the End (1 Thess. 5:1-4).

The interesting thing about these attempts to locate the dominant influence on Paul is that while no one of them succeeds in accounting for Paul, all of them have seen something that is really there. In other words, Paul was influenced by all these factors, some more than others. Exactly how they fit together logically will probably continue to elude students of Paul. The point is that he lived in a syncretistic era; it would be surprising if he did not represent something of an amalgam himself.

Several things need to be borne in mind for the interpretation of such a figure for religious and theological ends. (a) The origin of this idea or that motif is of interest to the historian trying to locate Paul in his own culture, but it was of no interest to Paul himself. Had anyone pointed out to him the "parallels" to his ideas and phrases, he may well have responded with imperial indifference. (b) Our labels tend to get in the way. Far too often it is assumed that if one of Paul's phrases sounds gnostic it could not at the same time be derived from Hellenized Judaism, that what has been identified as rabbinic should not be found among apocalyptists. Label like gnostic, Hellenistic Jewish, Stoic, apocalyptic, do not mark off fixed boundaries but merely identify the range within which one seeks family resemblances of ideas. In antiquity ideas did not flow in pipes. (c) The religious and theological validity of Paul's ideas in no way depends on how one judges their antecedents and parallels in antiquity. An idea does not necessarily become more significant or adequate when one can show that it was more at home in Judaism than in Hellenism, though some discussions imply that ideas are valid only if they have been circumcised.

Scholars have sometimes written of Paul's "borrowing" ideas, as if he consciously blended them. This is exceedingly doubtful, though we shall see that he could adopt the language of his readers in order to argue with them on their own turf. The question of "backgrounds" is at least as important for getting a profile of the readers as it is for Paul. In this light, Paul's letters represent the interaction, and sometimes the collision, of somewhat diverse backgrounds. To understand this, we need a clear picture of the nature of Paul's letters. That will be the focus of the next chapter.

CHAPTER TWO

THE THEOLOGY OF PAUL AND THE THEOLOGY OF THE LETTERS

It is a commonplace to say that it is easier to interpret Paul than Jesus because we have direct access to Paul's own letters but only indirect access to Jesus through the Gospels. Even so, the theology of Paul and the theology expressed in the letters are not identical. This is not because Paul thought one thing and wrote another; rather, this distinction results from the character of Paul's letters as we know them. What we know of Paul's theology depends on *the letters we have*; yet the letters themselves were significantly affected by what lay *ahead* of them (among the readers), and by what lay *behind* them (in the writer and his resources) as well. Each of these will be explored in this chapter.

THE CHARACTER OF PAUL'S LETTERS

The *first* thing to see is that Paul's letters come to us as a collection made and accepted by the church as "The Letters of Paul." Today scholarly judgment has distinguished genuine from non-genuine letters within this collection (see chapter 1), but the collection itself represents the ancient church's attempt to do the same thing, for the church excluded the Letter to the Laodiceans (now lost), so-called 3 Corinthians, and the exchange of brief letters between Paul and the philosopher Seneca. In other words, the concern to identify which letters claiming to be from Paul are genuine and which are secondary is as old as the canon. The author of 2 Thessalonians had to warn the readers about another "Pauline" letter claiming that Paul taught that the Day of the Lord had already come (2 Thess. 2:2; a similar point was combated in 2 Tim. 2:16–18). When modern critical judgment concludes that 2 Thessalonians itself is non-genuine, it is simply extending and refining the process which began even before the original collection was formed.

The Pauline collection not only includes more than Paul himself wrote but also less than everything he produced. We know of letters which have disappeared. In 1 Cor. 5:9 Paul refers to a letter which was misunderstood, at least in part, and which Paul now explains. The theory that part of this letter is now embedded in 2 Corinthians, at 6:14-7:1, has not persuaded all students. Further, 2 Cor. 2:4 mentions a letter written with intense anguish; part of it appears to be included in 2 Corinthians (chapters 10-13), but part of it also appears to be lost. Col. 4:16 refers to a letter "from Laodicea," evidently one that will come from there to Colossae. Even if Paul did not write Colossians, a matter of continuing dispute, there is no reason to doubt that there once circulated a letter to the Laodiceans. (The brief "Letter to the Laodiceans" which we do have is certainly a different work, for it is merely a pastiche of Pauline phrases.)

More important, Paul's letters were also edited. Of the seven undoubtedly genuine letters, only in the case of Philemon can we be certain that what we have is virtually identical with what Paul wrote. In a few cases, the manuscripts reveal this editorial work. For example, the concluding benediction of Romans appears at 16:25-27 in most manuscripts, but p^{46} has it after 15:33, some after 14:23, some at both places, and others omit it altogether. Evidently different editions were prepared for church use.

Usually, however, the evidence for editorial work is internal, not disclosed by manuscript differences. For instance, Phil. 1:1 mentions bishops and deacons. Since it appears that our Philippians is a compilation of shorter letters, one suspects that here the editor has updated the greeting to include church officials; apart from this reference, there is no indication that such offices existed during Paul's own time.

The most common evidence for editing is tension in content or difficult transitions from one part to another. A few examples will illustrate both. (a) Where the transitions from one paragraph to another are inexplicably abrupt, it is almost certain that here an editor juxtaposed parts of two letters. For instance, at Phil. 3:1

(and in the foregoing lines) Paul strikes a note of joy, but at 3:2 the text shifts to a bitter warning: "Look out for the dogs, look out for the evil-workers," etc. This tone continues through the rest of chap. 3, but at 4:1 the theme of joy returns. In other words, 3:2–21 is part of another letter. Our 2 Corinthians is also widely regarded as composite. We already noted that 2 Cor. 6:14–7:1 is part of another letter; to test this, one has only to read 7:2 after 6:13 to see that without the intervening material the text reads smoothly and reasons coherently.

(b) Sometimes the tensions between parts of a present letter are not so clearly related to abrupt transitions, but nonetheless suggest, to some students at least, that an editor has been rather skillful in joining parts of diverse letters. One example is 2 Corinthians 8 and 9, both of which deal with the collection of funds for Jerusalem, but from different points of view. A less obvious instance is 1 Corinthians 8–10, where some students see parts of different letters because in chapter 8 Paul argues that since idols have no existence, food that had been offered to them in a token ritual may be eaten by Christians unless doing so offends a "weak" brother. In chapter 10, he seems to argue that because pagan sacrifice is actually offered to demons, Christians cannot participate in cult meals of both the pagan shrines and the church. On the other hand, many interpreters see only a refinement of the argument in chapter 8, not evidence that chapter 10 is a later, different letter-fragment.

Given the nature of the evidence and the role of personal judgment about what is too different to have been written in the same letter, it is inevitable that proposals to factor 1, 2 Corinthians and Philippians into component parts have differed considerably among themselves. Some more cautious students have therefore concluded that such proposals cancel one another and have refused to grant that these letters are composite. However, neither the fallibility of a given reconstruction nor the diversity of proposals disallows the main point—that at least 2 Corinthians and Philippians are compiled. The point is that what we have are those forms of Paul's letters which were prepared for church use long after Paul himself wrote them.

Another phenomenon appears from time to time in these letters —the addition of brief statements, sometimes phrases, to the text. These are of two kinds, interpolations (new material) and glosses (interpretive comments originally made in the margin, then incorporated by a copiest). It is not always possible to differentiate precisely what is gloss and what is interpolation, but many of these brief post-Pauline additions have been detected. Because good manuscripts often include them, the additions were made very early. Several of these interpolations have been rather influential, unfortunately. One is 1 Thess. 2:14–16, where the text regards the fall of Jerusalem (the probable referent) as God's punishment on the Jews for killing Jesus and persecuting Christians. Another is 1 Cor. 14:33b–36, which forbids women to speak in church worship. Not only does this contradict 1 Cor. 11:5, which assumes that women do pray and prophesy in church, but it also agrees with the post-Pauline author of 1 Tim. 2:11–12. So Paul has been blamed for a view that he did not have.

We may summarize: *First,* (a) we do not have access to Paul's letters as he wrote them, but only to the letters as they were incorporated into a collection. (b) Several of our letters combine parts of different letters, written on different occasions but presumably to the same readers. (c) Secondary materials were added here and there, and some parts of letters omitted. The conclusion is clear: the letters of Paul as we have them cannot be simply equated with what Paul himself wrote. What the letters present us with is Paul as he was transmitted by the church. This is one reason why the theology of the letters is not simply identical with the theology of Paul himself.

Second, Paul wrote letters that were occasional—occasioned by particular circumstances in his churches. None of his letters was written simply as a means of self-expression and then shared with friends, the way some persons write poetry as a hobby. Nor were the letters written for the general public, as if produced for publication and sale to a "religious market." Rather, they were written for particular congregations (small house churches) who had particular problems. (To some extent Romans is an exception because Paul had not yet been to Rome; for a discussion see Donfried, *The Romans Debate.*) The particularity of each occasion accounts for the diversity among the letters.

Several aspects of the occasional character of Paul's letters deserve mention. (a) Because the letters are Paul's responses to what was going on among the readers, it is necessary to understand the situation to which the letters respond. (b) However, all we can know of the situation must be inferred from the answer; we have no independent, non-Pauline, access to the situation. After inferring the question we can interpret the answer. There is no alternative to such circular reasoning. (c) One must assume that Paul did not misunderstand or misrepresent the situation. This very point has been challenged by Schmithals, who contended that, at least to begin with, Paul misunderstood the problem in Corinth, with the result that his answer in 1 Corinthians 15 was partly misplaced (*Gnosticism in Corinth*; e.g., pp. 155-6). However, Paul was much closer to the Corinthians than is Schmithals, or any other modern. (d) Paul's understanding of the issues did not necessarily coincide with what the readers themselves thought. The Galatians, for instance, thought that accepting circumcision would make them first class Christians, but Paul thought it would nullify the Christian faith altogether. (e) Even if we were to "add up" all the letters, they would not contain everything that Paul believed or thought. Rather, the result would be a compend of things Paul deemed necessary to say to a spectrum of issues. Because Paul addressed "pressure points" in his churches, he needed only to mention other matters which he did not regard as problematic. What was not in dispute could be assumed, such as using the Bible of the synagogue as Scripture also for the church.

The occasional character of Paul's letters calls for a measure of sensitivity on the part of the interpreter. To interpret them calls for more than making their contents intelligible; it includes making Paul's point in a manner that confronts today's readers in a way analogous to what occurred originally. To facilitate this, the interpreter needs to penetrate not only Paul's "answer" but also the "question" until what becomes apparent is the extent to which today's readers share the same problem as the original ones. The greater the similarity, the more directly Paul's response may address also our own. For example, if today "tongue speaking" disrupts a congregation and leads to a certain pride on the part of those who have this capacity, then Paul's word in 1 Corinthians 12–14 can be as pertinent today as then. If the interpreter first finds the particularity of the original occasions to be an obstacle to appropriating Paul, it is probably because one expects the letters to articulate timeless truths and principles to be applied, rather than timely words to concrete situations which are prototypes of our own. In other words, in the long run it is precisely the particularity of the occasions that makes Paul's letters perennially significant.

The *third* characteristic of Paul's letters concerns their formal elements, what one might call their components, and their mode of argument. It has long been recognized that Paul's letters both adopt and adapt the letter-writing conventions of the time. The Greek letter had three elements: an introductory statement (name of sender and recipient, greetings, a word of thanks to the gods, and sometimes a wish that the gods aid the recipient), the body of the letter containing the subject-matter to be communicated, and the conclusion (final greetings to mutual acquaintances, closing prayer-wish to the gods, sometimes the date). In recent years, scholars have studied the formal elements (stereotyped phrases, conventions of moving from one part to another, etc.) and types of letters (letters of recommendation, personal correspondence, official letters, etc.) rather intensely, drawing especially on a mass of letters written on papyrus. Doty's *Letters in Primitive Christianity* provides an excellent overview of the results.

By analyzing Graeco-Roman letters (Greek, Latin, Hebrew, Aramaic) we understand Paul's letter-writing better. To begin with, Paul's letters were not dashed off spontaneously, nor were they private correspondence; the first great student of the papyri letters, Adolf Deissmann, argued for both of these points, but wrongly. Deissmann, moreover, distinguished too sharply the letter (personal, spontaneous, informal correspondence) from the epistle, a self-conscious literary production designed for publication. Paul's letters actually combine features of both. They embody Paul's intense personal involvement in the issues but they were also designed to be read (aloud) in the congregations (1 Thess. 5:27; Philem. 2). Paul apparently wrote these letters when he could not personally visit the congregations. He regarded his letters as "stand-ins" for his own presence. When a letter from Paul was read, it was as though Paul himself were speaking. Moreover, Paul clearly wrote out of his sense of apostolic authority. Paul did not see himself expressing merely personal opinions and preferences, but as articulating the normative meaning of the revelation of God in Jesus Christ. The letter to Philemon shows how Paul could write short personal letters, though Philem. 2 implies that he expected also it to be shared with the church.

Second, we have learned that Paul carefully structured his letters, and modified letter-writing conventions at certain points. (a) The standard greeting (A to B, Greetings!) becomes more elaborate. Except in the case of Romans and Galatians, Paul mentions associates. This makes it clear that the letter is not private correspondence. Moreover, he states his apostolic authorization (1, 2 Corinthians, Galatians) when that is a factor in the situation being addressed; otherwise he characterizes himself as a slave of Christ (Philippians) or as a prisoner (Philemon). In Romans he combines these modes of self-introduction: "Paul, a slave of Christ Jesus, a called apostle" and then elaborates, "set apart for the gospel of God." The Galatian situation prompted him to defend his apostleship in the first line, "not from men nor through man but through Jesus Christ and God the Father. . . ." Thus Paul's modifications of the greetings alert the reader to the content to follow. The concluding element of the Greek greeting (chairein = "Greeting") Paul modified to grace (charis) and peace, the latter reflecting the Jewish shalom.

(b) In place of a phrase thanking the gods for his own good health, Paul developed a distinctive paragraph of thanksgiving (found in all his letters except Galatians because the crisis was so severe that Paul could not give thanks) in which he expressed gratitude for the vitality of the Christian faith among the readers. Moreover, the thanksgiving paragraph often modulates into an eschatological chord; thereby Paul reminded the readers that salvation would be completed at the parousia (the coming of Christ). Furthermore, the thanksgiving subtly announces themes to be developed in the body of the letter. Thus Rom. 1:11–12 tactfully speaks of Paul's desire to share a spiritual gift with the Romans, and the following verses (12–17) show that what he wants to share is his understanding of the gospel, whose formulation climaxes the whole paragraph and so announces the theme of the entire letter. The interpreter of Paul's letters finds important clues by attending to the carefully composed paragraphs of thanksgiving.

(c) The body of the letter develops the themes. Because this part of the letter is so much longer than the comparable part of the ordinary Greek letter, there is reason to regard Paul's letters as "letter-essays" or "instructional letters." Since this part of the letter responds most directly to the issues among the readers, there is considerable diversity in the body of the various letters. Nonetheless, three features appear to be common to them all: One, subsections tend to build toward an eschatological note. Two, Paul includes his travel plans (Rom. 15:14–33; 1 Cor. 4:14–21; 1 Corinthians 16; 2 Cor. 12:14–13:13; Gal. 4:12–20; Phil. 2:19–24; Philem. 21–22). Were the readers persistently curious about Paul's itinerary? Not necessarily. Funk has linked these passages with Paul's sense of apostolic authority; they constitute a peculiar element in Paul's letters because they deal with the "apostolic parousia"—Paul's authoritative presence ("The Apostolic *Parousia*: Form and Significance," in *Christian History and Interpretation,* ed. by Farmer, Moule, and Niebuhr, pp. 249–68). Three, exhortations (technically called *paraenesis*) usually appear near the end. The paraenesis includes a variety of topics not directly related to the argument. This is partly because Paul draws on traditions of moral counsel which touch a range of topics, and partly because Paul thinks certain admonitions are called for. The range of topics can be seen in Romans 12–13 or 1 Thess. 5:12–22.

(d) Paul also changes the letter-closing. In place of the wish for good health followed by "Farewell!" (*errose*) Paul puts benedictions and doxologies. Both are rooted in the tradition of Jewish and emerging Christian worship—another indication of Paul's expectation that the letters would be read in worship. Several letters ask that readers greet one another with the "holy kiss" (Rom. 16:16; 1 Cor. 16:20; 2 Cor. 13:12; 1 Thess. 5:26). The concluding greetings to readers (sometimes named) were customary. Also customary is Paul's taking the stylus into his own hands to add a final note (1 Cor. 16:21–24; Gal. 6:11; Philem. 19). No trace of an original date remains; those given in some manuscripts are later guesses.

The fact that Paul calls attention to what he himself writes reminds us that he probably dictated his letters. In only one instance do we know the scribe's name (Rom. 16:22). We do not know whether Paul dictated word for word, or whether he told his scribe what to say but left the wording up to him. Paul sent the letter by personal courier, who probably also read it to the church and commented as he went along. There is a hint of this in Eph. 6:21–22 and Col. 4:7–8. When Paul's letters are read and interpreted in Christian worship, they are being used in their native habitat. Paul's letters are as at home in worship as a play is on stage.

The fact that Paul dictated his letters knowing that they would be read aloud to the house church explains why the letters contain so many rhetorical features. Scholars are resuming the analysis of the rhetorical character of Paul's letters. This work focuses on the body of the letter, where the arguments are developed. Long ago Bultmann called attention to Paul's use of the rhetorical form developed by the Cynic-Stoic street preachers—the *diatribē*. Here the speaker addressed an imaginary opponent, whose counter-question set up the next point to be made by the speaker (somewhat like a "straight man" in a stand-up comedy). Rom. 3:27–31 is a good example. At such passages, the interpreter should not conclude that Paul is answering actual objections raised by specific (though unnamed) opponents among the readers. Of course, Paul may have formulated the objections in light of his experience in debates.

Formal analysis of the Pauline letters is also concerned with the kind of argument Paul constructs overall. As such work progresses, the nature of Paul's letters as literary/rhetorical wholes will come into sharper focus. In the long run, comparing Paul's letters with ancient rhetoric may be more important than comparing them with ancient letters.

THE FOREGROUND OF THE LETTERS

Just as there is a continuing debate over which aspect of Paul's cultural background was most significant (see chapter 1), so there is an ongoing discussion over the nature of the problems with which Paul contended and over the persons who generated them. Nor is it clear whether the difficulties in local congregations were expressions of a single phenomenon, or whether Paul had to contend with quite different and unrelated problems.

For the interpreter the advantages of finding a single front are as clear as are the difficulties which result from finding multiple fronts; that is, the more unified the issues the more coherent and unified Paul's theological response. Conversely, the more diverse the issues, the greater the difficulty of finding a common core. This is why the question before us has a direct bearing on the way Paul's theology is portrayed.

Those who, following the lead of Baur (see chapter 1), find the key to Paul's theology in his tension with Jewish Christianity see the pervasive foreground in the trouble stirred up by Judaizers. The term "Judaizers" does not appear in the NT itself but is formed from the verb "Judaize" (Gal. 2:14; RSV: "live like a Jew"). Judaizers were Jewish Christians who insisted that gentile believers must join the ethnic community of Israel in order to be bonafide Christians. How could one believe that Jesus is the Messiah and not be part of the Messiah's people? Paul, however, insisted that everyone becomes a member of the holy community by faith; thereby he redefined that community. Jewish Christians regarded Paul, therefore, as propagating a distorted gospel, and he returned the compliment.

The conflict came to a head before Paul wrote the letters we have, and was to have been settled at "the Jerusalem Council" (Acts 15 and Galatians 2). These differing accounts agree on the main point—male gentile Christians were not required to be circumcised—a rite by which one became a full-fledged Jew. Even though Paul's gospel was acknowledged by the Council, problems continued because it had not been decided whether Jewish and gentile Christians could eat together. Some Jewish Christians arrived in Antioch and hectored the Jewish Christians so that they segregated themselves. Not even Peter and Barnabas, Paul's associates, could withstand the pressure. Paul reports all this to the Galatians because later the gentile Christians in Galatia were being persuaded to accept circumcision. Unfortunately for us, Paul did not identify who it was that was derailing the Galatians (he didn't have to; everybody then knew who it was); Gal. 6:12–13 is an intriguing characterization of them, but we still do not know who these people were or whether they had come from Jerusalem.

Phil. 3:2–21 shows that Paul was contending with persons who took pride in their Jewishness and insisted on circumcision. 2 Corinthians 10–13 indicates that Paul's opposition in Corinth was Jewish (2 Cor. 11:22), though the word "circumcision" does not appear. Because in Romans Paul developed so fully his theology of justification by faith (apart from the law), one might infer that "Judaizers" got to Rome before Paul and had already discredited his gospel (see, e.g., Rom. 3:8, 31). In this way the conflict with "Judaizers" can be traced throughout the letters, and be made the single front against which Paul's theology was written.

Those who find the key to Paul's theology in his struggle with an early form of Gnosticism find some kind of gnostic under every bed. Such pan-Gnosticism has been advocated especially by Schmithals. He flatly denies that the instigators of the problem in Galatia were in any way dependent on Jerusalem Christianity (*Paul and the Gnostics,* p. 25); the challenge to Paul's apostleship does not come from that quarter but from gnostics who claim divine revelations. Those who were undermining Paul wherever he went were Jewish Christian gnostics from Asia Minor. The same gnostics who disdained Paul in Galatia and in Corinth were active also in Philippi. Since "no Judaizers emerged on the scene against Paul . . . Baur's construction of the history is dissolved" (*ibid.,* p. 117).

Another way of positing continuity in the issues has been advocated by Käsemann (in numerous publications). His over-arching term is "enthusiasm," a somewhat elusive concept. By "enthusiasm" Käsemann means more a stance than a particular group or theology. This stance emphasizes the radical newness of the Christian life, celebrates the "already" of salvation to the detriment of the "not yet," revels in the Spirit and regards the sacraments as guarantees of salvation. Although Käsemann sees some sort of enthusiasm as endemic to Christianity from the start, what interests him is its development in Paul's Hellenistic churches, for which Corinth serves as the model. Paul himself cannot be isolated from it; indeed, he came into conflict with Palestinian Christians because "he had become the champion of the enthusiastic Hellenistic churches which were growing up free of the Law" (*Perspectives on Paul*, p. 125). Yet Paul was also intensely critical of enthusiasm when it became one-sided, and he relied on apocalyptic to counterweight it. In other words, Käsemann sees Paul as fighting against both enthusiasm and Judaistic legalism (*New Testament Questions of Today*, p. 254). By appealing to "enthusiasm" Käsemann penetrates to a deeper issue, the claim of all first century Christians to be living in the power of the New Age; this claim in turn was expressed in various theologies and life-styles. "Enthusiasm" allows Käsemann to incorporate the insight of the history of religion— that Hellenistic Christianity was deeply influenced by its environment through mystery cults, metaphysical dualism of body and spirit, and the myth of the divine redeemer—yet without simply making the Corinthians into gnostic Christians. Most important, by allowing Paul to share enthusiasm Käsemann anchors him firmly in Hellenistic Christianity; at the same time Käsemann regards Paul as its internal critic, always striving for a right balance between the "already" and the "not yet." Thus Paul becomes the great forerunner of the Reformation theme of *simul justus et peccator* (simultaneously justified and a sinner).

Several conclusions can be drawn from this sketch. (a) Inevitably the problems at Corinth have dominated the discussion. Not only does the sheer bulk of the Corinthian letters provide more evidence, but factoring out a number of earlier letters allows one to trace the history of Paul's problem in Corinth in a way that cannot be done elsewhere. Once a profile of the Corinthian church emerges, it is easy to find traces of the same problem elsewhere. However, it is far from clear that the issues remained the same even in Corinth. In 1 Corinthians the problems appear to be less severe than in 2 Corinthians 10–13, where it seems that outsiders have made matters worse. The actual situation was probably much more fluid and diverse than we can determine. If this was true of Corinth, it is probably true also of Paul's other churches. It is interesting to note that most attempts to unify the front against which Paul fought often have trouble integrating 1 Thessalonians into the argument. (b) Despite the danger of claiming to know too much, the value of such studies for the interpreter of Paul is clear. Negatively, they guard one against visualizing Paul as writing his theology out of his own musings, just as they prevent one from treating the occasion of the letters as a mere catalyst which triggered Paul's thinking. Positively, these efforts allow us to see Paul at work, struggling with alternate interpretations of the gospel being advocated by real people. Paul himself emerges as an intensely human apostle, and his theology as a dynamic process constantly interacting with the stance of Christians just as committed as he was.

THE BACKGROUND OF THE LETTERS

Just as Paul's foreground determined what he had to discuss, so his background affected how he would say it and the resources at his disposal. The theology of the letters articulates the specific interaction of these elements; the rest of Paul's theology remains largely hidden from us, apart from allusions. Because the multiple cultural background of Paul was noted in chapter 1, we will concentrate here on his personal background, and his use of traditions.

Although some scholars have doubted that Paul had been a student of Gamaliel in Jerusalem (Acts 22:3) it is impossible to doubt the statement in Acts 26:5—that Paul had been a Pharisee —because Paul himself confirms it (Phil. 3:5; Gal. 1:14). Precisely what "Pharisee" meant in Paul's case is not self-evident because of two considerations: one, he was a diaspora Jew who according to Acts (16:37; 22:28) was a Roman citizen from birth; his letters always use his Roman name, Paulus. Two, Pharisaism in Paul's early years differed from the rabbinism which developed after the fall of Jerusalem in A.D. 70; hence one must be cautious in using second century rabbinic texts to describe pre-70 Pharisaism. Nonetheless, it is certain that he had been a Pharisee, zealous for the Torah.

Equally important, Paul remembers that he had tried to destroy Christianity. Curiously, he never reveals what prompted him to undertake that project (1 Cor. 15:9; Gal. 1:13). Since Judaism seems to have tolerated a rather broad spectrum of beliefs, including views of who the Messiah would be, it is unlikely that what set Paul into motion was only the belief that the Messiah was Jesus. It is more likely that Paul saw the developing freedom with regard to the law, especially among the Hellenistic Jewish Christians, as a threat to Judaism and as an affront to God. Then he turned around: the persecutor became propagator. Paul never describes his "conversion," though he refers to it as a revelation of God's Son (Gal. 1:16); nor does he tell us where or when it occurred. All discussion of his "Damascus road" experience depends on Acts (9:1–19; 22:4–16; 26:9–18).

Paul did not separate the experience of coming to faith from knowing himself to be called by God to be an apostle to the gentiles. His conversion and his call coincided (Gal. 1:15–16). Because Paul did not have this experience as the result of an extended religious quest, nor under the tutelage of a mentor or guru, he regarded his coming to faith as an act of God, as divine intervention to rescue a persecutor from self-destruction. It was an act of God's grace. This meant that Paul also regarded his gospel as divinely authorized, as the Word of God (1 Thess. 2:13). To challenge Paul's gospel was to challenge his authorization, his warrant; to challenge his warrant was to challenge his gospel. So intimate was the connection between the man and the message that Paul insisted that his apostolic status was dependent on God only (Gal. 1:1, 12); he was Christ's own apostle, not a legate or emissary of the church. He believed God himself was calling his hearers to faith through his word (2 Cor. 5:20). It is essential to see that for Paul it is not he who legitimates his gospel (it is true because it is Paul's), but it is the gospel which legitimates Paul (Paul is an apostle because the gospel is true).

Sometimes Paul's theology has been regarded as simply an explication of his experience. This is as difficult to deny as it is to demonstrate. The former because it is hard to sunder the man from the message, the latter because Paul never grounds his theological arguments in his conversion experience. Only rarely does he refer to his religious experiences of any kind (1 Cor. 9:1; 2 Cor. 12:1–10; Gal. 1:12–17; 2:2), and all of these are in polemical discussion in which he defends his authorization. Nor does Paul say that his theology was revealed to him (1 Thess. 4:15 might imply this, but might also refer to a tradition). Though he can speak in tongues, he does not regard his letters as "translations" of what he heard or uttered in ecstasy. Nonetheless, a Pharisee whose zeal led him to persecute a new faith among fellow Jews, and who then turned about and advocated what he had tried to destroy, and who regarded this transformation as God's act—such a person can scarcely develop any other kind of theology than one which emphasized the radicality of God's grace and power.

Difficult as it is to discern precisely how Paul's conversion experience is linked to this theological thinking, it is even more difficult to see how his apostolic experience affected his thought. The time span between Paul's conversion (around A.D. 35) and the earliest letter we have (around A.D. 50/51) is greater than the period during which the letters we know were written (ca. A.D. 51–57, assuming that no parts of our Philippians were written from Rome). This earlier period is totally hidden from us, yet it probably consisted of the same sort of activities which we see later: traveling in dangerous circumstances, teaching in synagogues where he was more often repudiated than not and where he was three times officially punished with 39 lashes, baptizing those who accepted his message, nurturing the new community in house churches by explaining the meaning of it all in light of the synagogue Bible—all the while working for a living (see 2 Cor. 11:23–29; 1 Thess. 2:1–12). The man who wrote the seven letters was no novice, but a seasoned teacher-pastor who had had ample occasion to develop a repertoire of phrases, arguments, and ways of appealing to Scripture. Even though Paul's letters respond to concrete situations, we need not think that every line is a fresh creation. It is likely that Paul reformulated and rethought things he had said before, perhaps often. This may account, in part, for the compact style in certain passages.

In short, the personal background of each letter is the entire career of Paul up to the moment of dictation. If the whole of Paul's thought is never visible, even in the aggregate, Paul himself is nonetheless authentically present, revealing a good deal about himself while rarely making himself the subject-matter of the letters.

The other factor in the background of the letters consists of the traditions which Paul used. Paul relied on older material more often than he indicated—1 Cor. 11:23-25 (the Lord's Supper) and 15:3-7 (resurrection appearances). In both cases he used fixed formulations and therefore introduced them with technical rabbinic terms for receiving and transmitting tradition. It is likely that he received these traditions when he became a member of the church, just as it is likely that the traditions themselves had been formulated by the Hellenistic Jewish Christians in Damascus or Antioch, who in turn relied, in part, on motifs and phrases used in Palestine.

Careful attention to vocabulary and rhythmic phrasing has led to the conclusion that Paul quoted material also at other points. There is broad consensus that Phil. 2:6-11 is a Christ-hymn, and that Rom. 1:3-5 contains a confession (or part of one). The same holds true of Rom. 3:25, though Rom. 4:25 may be Paul's own rhetorically-balanced formulation. Rom. 10:9 also looks like a traditional formulation, as does Gal. 3:20-21. 1 Corinthians 13 is often regarded as an "ode to love" which Paul found appropriate to use here. 1 Cor. 15:33; 2 Cor. 9:6, and Gal. 5:9 are proverbs, and 1 Cor. 15:32 is a popular slogan that looks like a parody of the Epicurean attitude toward death. 1 Cor. 3:17a has been called a "sentence of holy law," identified by Käsemann as a retribution formula used by early Christian prophets (*New Testament Questions of Today*, pp. 66-81). Rom. 1:29-31 is a list of vices probably taken from Hellenized Judaism; comparable lists are found in popular moral literature of the time. The same is true of 1 Cor. 6:9-10. 1 Thess. 4:13-5:11 is an extended piece of apocalyptic instruction. Paul's ethical injunctions probably use pieces of tradition characterized by terse imperatives (Rom. 12:9-21; 2 Cor.

13:11; 1 Thess. 5:14–22). There are also instances where Paul used inherited exegetical materials; one example is the string of OT quotations in Rom. 3:10–18. (Paul's use of the words of Jesus will concern us in chapter 4.)

In the last decade, there has been a clear upsurge in efforts to identify not only post-Pauline additions to the texts but also Paul's own dependence on earlier materials. Indeed, in a few cases such as Rom. 3:24–26 or 1 Thess. 2:14–16, what one person regards as pre-Pauline tradition another calls an interpolation. This is partly because in both cases the evidence—differing vocabulary and point of view—for the one can be adduced also on behalf of the other hypothesis. What tips the scale in favor of Paul's own use of earlier material is the extent to which it is integral to the argument. The more integrated, the stronger the likelihood that Paul himself included it. The same consideration, however, makes it difficult to distinguish when Paul's own language draws on earlier material (as in a paraphrase) from when he simply incorporates sentences congenial with his own thought. It would be easier to factor the Pauline letters into three strata—pre-Pauline, Pauline, and post-Pauline—if we had a more precise use of the word "tradition," and if it were used consistently. In what follows, "tradition" will be reserved for *traditum*—what has been handed down in a stable formulation; "traditional" will be used for passages where one suspects that Paul is not creating fresh sentences but drawing on inherited (and perhaps common) phrases or motifs.

For example, in 1 Cor. 15:27–28 Paul interprets Ps. 110:1, widely used by early Christians to interpret Jesus' exaltation in resurrection. The inferences drawn from this psalm are Paul's own, but associating the psalm with Jesus' resurrection was "traditional," customary. Likewise in 1 Cor. 10:4 Paul Christianizes a rabbinic interpretation of two stories in the OT (Exod. 17:1–7; Num. 20:1–13). Jewish exegetes had inferred that although both stories refer to a wondrous rock, there was only one rock, and therefore the rock followed the Israelites. Paul assumes all this, and simply identifies the rock as Christ. In cases like this, the tacit understandings are traditional, but what appears in Paul's letters are not pieces of fixed tradition, but his own free use of inherited motifs.

Discovering the great extent to which Paul adopted and adapted pieces of tradition, traditional modes of thought, and motifs helps the interpreter overcome the notion—ultimately grounded in Romanticism—that Paul was a solitary, original genius who created his theological understanding out of his own depths. Paul's "depths" were indeed plumbed as he wrote, but his creativity consisted largely in his capacity to give traditions and traditional material new significance by expounding their implications for the crises he confronted. Paul was a bearer and refractor of multiple traditions and inherited motifs. In the deutero-Pauline letters we see how Paul himself became traditional material for the next generation.

Paul's clear reliance on earlier materials is one important side of the theme, "Paul and tradition." The other side concerns his freedom. This manifests itself not only in the wide range of resources upon which he drew, Christian and non-Christian, but also in his freedom to modify and reinterpret what he used. It is widely believed, for instance, that he added "even death on a cross" to the hymn in Phil. 2:8 (and perhaps other phrases as well). In 1 Cor. 11:26 he comments on the Lord's Supper tradition, and in 1 Cor. 15:8 he does not hesitate to add his own name to the roster of those to whom Christ appeared. Likewise he seems to have expanded the confessional formula in Rom. 1:3–5 and 3:24–26. For Paul, this older material was not a holy object to be handed on with reverence like a talisman; nor is Paul bound by earlier formulations as if they had been revealed. Rather, he moves among these multiple traditions with sovereign freedom. The letters show what happened when these materials passed through the mind of Paul.

PART II

THE GOSPEL PAUL PREACHED

How Paul preached the gospel when he arrived in a town remains largely unknown. The Book of Acts gives two sample sermons, one of his preaching in Hellenistic synagogues (Acts 13:13–41), the other of his preaching to gentile intellectuals (Acts 17:22–31). Since both fit so neatly the perspective of Acts, only with great caution can one use them to portray Paul's own preaching. That must be inferred from his letters.

The letters do not summarize what Paul preached to elicit faith, but interpret aspects of that preaching and its foundations. In developing his arguments, he alludes to this prior preaching/teaching; these references furnish the foundation of any reconstruction of Paul's preaching. To them we can add the traditions and traditional materials, motifs, and arguments which we noted in the foregoing chapter because readers would have recognized some of this material as part of Paul's earlier teaching.

We shall discuss three themes: the pivotal event of Jesus Christ (chapter 3); the salvific response which Paul elicited (chapter 4), and the theological horizons of his proclamation (chapter 5). A sharp distinction between the gospel Paul preached and the theological issues he developed and defended in the letters cannot be maintained, of course. Nonetheless, two things should emerge from these chapters: One, a sketch of Paul's message; two, an outline of the sub-stratum on which the epistles rest.

CHAPTER THREE

THE PIVOTAL EVENT

Paul called his message "gospel," *euangelion*; our word "evangelist" comes from the same word-family, yet Paul never calls himself an evangelist. His customary self-designation is "apostle," a sent-one—one sent by God to preach the gospel. It was the gospel that lay at the core of his self-understanding and of his life work (1 Thess. 2:4). Everything else was subservient to it.

Apparently it was Paul who introduced the term *euangelion* into the Christian vocabulary. Etymologically, *euangelion* is good news. *Euangelion* was not a common religious term in antiquity, neither among Greeks nor Jews. Interestingly, an inscription uses it in connection with the cult of the emperor: "The birthday of the god [the emperor] was for the world the beginning of good announcements" (the plural of *euangelion*). It is disputed whether this meaning influenced early Christian usage; in any case, for Christians there is only one *euangelion*. The plural is never used of the proclamation. The LXX (the Greek translation of the Bible made in Alexandria several centuries before Paul) uses the verb for announcements of God's eschatological deed, the coming of salvation (as quoted in Rom. 10:15, for example). How the noun *euangelion* got into Paul's vocabulary remains obscure, but the fact that he could write simply of "the gospel" shows that he assumed his readers knew what he was talking about (see e.g., Rom. 10:16; 1 Cor. 15:1). Paul uses *euangelion* more than any other NT writer.

Paul sometimes characterizes this gospel. When he calls it "the gospel of God" (Rom. 1:1; 2 Cor. 11:7; 1 Thess. 2:2), he means both the gospel which comes from God and the gospel about God, for the two cannot be separated neatly. When he calls it "the gospel of Christ" (e.g., Rom. 15:19; 1 Cor. 9:12; 2 Cor. 2:12;

10:14; 1 Thess. 3:2), however, he does not refer to Christ's own message but to the message whose content is Christ. When Paul writes of "my [or 'our'] gospel" (Rom. 2:16; 16:25; 2 Cor. 4:3; 1 Thess. 1:5) he does not imply that he has a message peculiar to himself, "his thing"; he simply means the gospel which he preached, as Gal. 1:11; 2:2 show. Precisely in this letter, where Paul must defend his gospel, he never calls it "my gospel," but insists that there is only one gospel (Gal. 1:6–8). Evidently Paul was convinced that theologies might differ, but there was only a single gospel. What his opponents later propagated in Galatia and Corinth was really "another gospel" (Gal. 1:7; 2 Cor. 11:4)—a self-contradiction sufficient to disqualify it.

Paul regarded his message as something radical and decisive, not as religious suggestions for better living, or as one more possibility alongside the many cults and religions of the day. Nor did Paul see himself propagating a new religion; whether in fact he was doing so is a modern historian's judgment. For Paul the gospel message was God's power that effected salvation (Rom. 1:16). Although it is an announcement of an event, it is not merely information about it. Although it is a word from and about God, and so is eminently theological, it is not merely theology either. Rather, the message itself has power wherever it is believed. Moreover, it was accompanied by events of power, what we might call "miracles" (2 Cor. 12:12; 1 Thess. 1:5), and by the powerful manifestations of God's Spirit among those who accepted the gospel and were baptized. Paul regarded these accompaniments as confirmation of the power of the message to transform human life. The gospel announced what God had done through the event we call "Jesus Christ." The remainder of this chapter will explore three aspects of Paul's gospel-presentation of the Christ-event: the cross-resurrection, the relation of Paul to Jesus and to the early tradition of Jesus' teachings, and finally Paul's understanding of the pre-existence of Christ.

CROSS AND RESURRECTION

The message which Paul preached to gentile hearers included an appeal to abandon the worship of the gods and "to serve a living and true God" (1 Thess. 1:9). This motif was shared with the

Jewish synagogue, as was the appeal to the OT as God's revelation. What distinguished Paul's message from that of the synagogue, and from that of other traveling preachers, was the way he presented the event of Jesus. This is clear in how Paul continues—"and to wait for his Son from heaven, whom he raised from the dead, Jesus who delivers us from the wrath to come." This passage is not a compendium of the themes of Paul's preaching; it highlights the future aspects of it in keeping with the problem to be addressed later, the Christian hope. Jesus is identified as God's Son who, having been raised from the dead and exalted to heavenly status, will come as deliverer from the great judgment ("the wrath to come"). In other words, the focus is on the salvific meaning of the Jesus-event, which is more than the lifetime of Jesus. In 1 Cor. 2:2, where Paul identified the focus of his preaching to the Corinthians, he wrote, "I decided to know nothing among you except Jesus Christ and him crucified"—clearly indicating the core was Christ and that Christ was presented from the angle of the crucifixion. The fact that 1 Thess. 1:10 (and Rom. 10:9, see pp. 27, 53) mentions only Jesus' resurrection, and 1 Cor. 2:2 only the cross does not mean that Paul shifted content; rather, because cross and resurrection constituted a single meaning-complex, he could mention one and imply the other, depending on which aspect was most germane to the point being made at the moment.

One of the most important texts in the NT is 1 Cor. 15:3–11, where Paul quotes a fixed tradition (see chapter 2): "Christ died for our sins in accordance with the scriptures, he was also buried and raised on the third day in accordance with the scriptures." This tradition was made the foundation of Paul's preaching in Corinth and elsewhere. Several things strike us about the way this old tradition speaks of the Jesus-event: (a) Since Christ means Messiah, the formulation expresses a drastic transformation of Jewish expectation. Attempts to find Jewish precedents for the idea that the Messiah would die to atone for sin have failed. (b) Christ's death is not understood as a tragedy that befell a good man, a miscarriage of justice, nor as a model of self-giving. Rather it is an event through which sin is effectively dealt with. (c) To say that both Christ's death and God's act of resurrecting him (the passive "was raised" implies that God did the resurrecting; Jesus did not "rise" from the dead) are in accord with Scripture is to call for a reexamination of Scripture, for a particular way of interpreting it. (d) Nothing is said about Christ's identity as God's Son, nor of the virgin birth, ministry, and teaching of Jesus. The focus is not on information about Jesus but on the salvific meaning of the event, focused on its outcome—death and resurrection.

That the core of Paul's preaching was Jesus' cross and resurrection as God's way of dealing with sin is clearly implied also by the way Paul writes to the Roman church which had not yet heard him preach. In this epistle Paul appropriates materials from Hellenistic Jewish Christianity, and assumes that the readers will recognize that his exposition of the gospel accords with those materials. Rom. 3:24–26 contains such traditional language. We need not decide precisely which phrases Paul inherited and which he contributed to the passage. Paul wrote of "the redemption which is in Christ Jesus, whom God has put forward as an expiation by his blood" (i.e., death). The word *hilastērion* (RSV: "expiation") can also be translated "mercy seat," an allusion to the lid of the sacred box, the ark of the covenant, in the Jerusalem temple. On the Day of Atonement this lid was sprinkled with sacrificial blood as part of the ritual by which God's forgiveness was granted and claimed. It is disputed whether Paul (or the tradition) meant "whom God put forward as a mercy seat by his blood"; probably "expiation" is correct. An expiation is not a propitiation. The latter is something that ameliorates wrath, dissolves hostility by placating the aggrieved; the former expunges, takes away sin. The point is that Christ's death does not do something that turns God's wrath away but something that deals with sin. The problem is not the disposition of God but the condition of humanity. This tightly compressed paragraph uses language taken from the Jewish sacrificial system to interpret Jesus' death as a sacrifice which deals with sin. How that occurs is not explained. In appropriating this tradition, Paul shows that he too understands Christ's death as atonement. The same is true of Rom. 4:24–25, which speaks of the resurrection of Jesus "who was put to death for our transgressions and raised for our justification." Here the RSV's "was put to death" translates *paredothē,* "was handed over" (by God). The same verb is used in the Lord's Supper tradition (1 Cor. 11:23), where the customary translation is "betrayed"; it could also be translated as "on the night when he was handed over" (by God, not by Judas).

What has emerged so far? Although the message which Paul presented in order to elicit faith included a variety of themes such as monotheism, Scripture, and the coming judgment, the core was the particular interpretation of the Jesus-event, and its focal point was the cross and resurrection. Just as Paul can oscillate between mentioning the cross and the resurrection without splitting them apart, so he can shift from saying that Christ gave himself (Gal. 1:4,20) to saying that God gave him over to death (Rom. 4:25). Christ's act was God's act: "God shows his love for us in that while we were yet sinners Christ died for us" (Rom. 5:8). This paradoxical way of speaking should not be glossed over, for together with the tradition in 1 Cor. 15:3, it expressed an understanding of God and Jesus which is constitutive for Paul's gospel (and for the type of Christianity in which it is rooted).

We do not know how the earliest Christians reasoned toward the formulations we now have in Paul's letters. Probably their starting point was not the incarnation but the resurrection. How might they have arrived at the convictions which are distilled in these formulations?

They did not begin in a vacuum, of course. As Jews, they already believed that sacrificial death and forgiveness of sins go together—an age-old connection. Given this assumption, they might have reasoned as follows: (a) God's resurrecting Jesus vindicates Jesus. (b) Those who believe that God has done this know themselves to be rightly related to God, forgiven; those who refuse to believe this are still at odds with God, though they think otherwise. (c) It is God's purpose that sin be dealt with and that persons be rightly related to himself. (d) Since the new right relation to God results from the resurrection, and since the resurrection would not have occurred apart from Jesus' death, Jesus' execution must be God's means of bringing about the new relationship. (e) Because to be granted a new relationship to God is to become the beneficiary of God's love, Christ's death must also be an act of his love, since precisely this new relationship to God would not have occurred apart from the cross/resurrection. (f) Consequently one can say that "Christ died for our sins." Whether or not these were the steps by which Christians came to the conclusions behind the tradition in 1 Corinthians 15 and Paul's statement in Rom. 5:8, these formulations are outcroppings of a rather sophisticated understanding of Jesus' death. The gospel is not theology, but it implies a particular theological understanding of God, Christ, and the human situation.

Paul's gospel was not presented simply as the answer to the religious quests of his hearers, but as the God-given announcement of an event whose meaning challenges those quests, at least the terms in which they were pursued. Paul characterized his gospel of the cross as "folly to those who are perishing"; it is a "stumbling-block to Jews and folly to Gentiles" (1 Cor. 1:18,22). The gospel challenged the prevailing understandings of God, the human condition, and the means of dealing with it; the gospel called for a reconstruction of those understandings.

PAUL AND THE TRADITIONS OF THE PIVOTAL EVENT

For Paul, the gospel is a heraldic announcement of an event, of a piece of history (the cross) inseparably linked with something that, strictly speaking, is not history at all—the resurrection. At the same time, in Paul's day there were circulating traditions about both Jesus' ministry and about the resurrection appearances. How was the gospel Paul preached related to these traditions?

Paul apparently never saw or heard Jesus (1 Cor. 9:1 refers to a vision of the resurrected Lord), and no one "saw" the resurrection. What Paul knew about Jesus depended either on reports and formulated traditions or on his immediate experience of the Lord. There were no written gospels in Paul's day. The collection of Jesus' sayings (Q) used by both Matthew and Luke was circulating then, probably in Palestine-Syria, but there is no reason to think that Paul used it. The question of Paul's relation to the Jesus-traditions has been debated intensely in Pauline study. We shall note the major positions taken after we have looked at Paul himself.

What did Paul know about Jesus' crucifixion and resurrection? (a) Paul says almost nothing about the crucifixion except that it occurred. None of the details which appear in any of our gospel accounts are mentioned by Paul—assuming that *paredothē* in 1 Cor. 11:23 means "handed over by God," not "betrayed" (i.e., by Judas). Since 1 Thess. 2:14–16 is an interpolation we cannot say that Paul blamed either the Jews or the Romans for the crucifixion. According to 1 Cor. 2:8, those who "crucified the Lord of glory" were "the rulers of this age"—apparently meaning that the invisible malign principalities and powers were at work in this event, using earthly agents. Paul has no interest in the earthly agents themselves (*we* connect them with Pilate and Caiaphas because we have the Gospels). When Paul mentions "Christ, our paschal lamb" (1 Cor. 5:7) he probably reflects knowledge that Christ's death occurred during Passover, but he gives no other information about the event itself. (b) Paul's knowledge of the resurrection is somewhat different. In 1 Cor. 15:8 he included himself in the tradition about those to whom the Lord was made visible; that makes him "an eyewitness" of the appearances, on a par with the others. But Paul never describes the Lord he saw. Nor does he ever mention the empty tomb. Nor does the list of appearances in the tradition quoted in 1 Corinthians 15 coincide with the appearance stories in the Gospels; the closest agreement is the trace of the fact that the Lord first appeared to Peter (Luke 24:34; Mark 16:7). It is sometimes said that because the tradition mentioned the burial (1 Cor. 15:4) Paul must have known that the tomb was empty because Jews could scarcely have believed otherwise if a buried man was resurrected. Yet the fact remains that Paul never mentions the tomb at all. We who have the Gospels have more resurrection traditions than Paul mentions, and some of those he mentions are not found in the Gospels (the appearance to the 500 and to James, Jesus' brother).

What did Paul know about Jesus prior to his execution? This is exceedingly difficult to determine, because all we know is what Paul mentions. Paul knew, of course, that Jesus was a Jew. According to Rom. 9:5, he was an Israelite, a descendant of Abraham according to Gal. 3:16, and a son of David according to Rom. 1:3.

He was born "under the law" (Gal. 4:4). Each of these references, however, is in the service of a theological point, and does not simply state a "historical fact." Paul also knew that Jesus had brothers (1 Cor. 9:5), one of whom was James, the head of the Jerusalem church (Gal. 1:19). That did not give James special standing in Paul's eyes, though he recognizes that this made James a "pillar" in the eyes of others (Gal. 2:6,9). Paul also knew that Jesus' mission was among his own people (Rom. 15:8), something that could be assumed. Paul never mentions the virgin birth, Jesus' baptism by John (though Acts 13:24–25 has him do so), nor any of the deeds of Jesus' ministry.

What did Paul know about Jesus' teaching? If we had only Paul's letters, we would never know that Jesus told parables, nor that he had preached the news of the kingdom. What strikes many students as especially problematic is that even when Paul writes about things which Jesus also discussed (e.g., food laws or taxes to Rome) Paul does not mention Jesus' teaching (Mark 7:1–23, which includes later material; 12:13–17). Even if Paul knew the Lord's Prayer (Rom. 8:15), he does not associate it with Jesus. What Paul does cite as Jesus' word is a saying about divorce (1 Cor. 7:10–11), support for preachers of the gospel (1 Cor. 9:14) and the coming of the Lord (1 Thess. 4:15–17). It is not clear whether "the word of the Lord" in 1 Thess. 4:15–17 is a tradition (or rests on traditional materials) from the pre-Easter Jesus or a word of the risen Lord. 1 Cor. 9:14 is not a quotation but a statement of the point: "Those who proclaim the gospel should get their living by the gospel," something that accords with Matt. 10:10 and Luke 10:7–8 but is not verbally identical with either one. In 1 Cor. 7:10–11, he knows the Markan form of Jesus' teaching which forbids both husband and the wife to divorce (Mark 10:10–12. Compare Matt. 5:31–32; 19:9; Luke 16:18). Paul also distinguishes sharply what the Lord says ("Not I but the Lord," v. 10) from what Paul himself says ("I say, not the Lord," v. 12), an indication that the tradition of the Lord's teaching is being taken very seriously.

This remarkable (to us!) absence of Jesus' teaching from Paul's letters, and of the total neglect of his ministry and the limited reference to his passion, has spawned various explanations which tend to be one of two types. The first regards the evidence of the letters as misleading and argues that Paul knew more, and valued what he knew, about Jesus than the letters show; the second regards the evidence of the letters as a quite accurate reflection of Paul's attitude. We will look briefly at both.

The attempt to show that the Jesus-traditions were actually more important to Paul than the number of references in the letters indicate is usually built on three considerations. One emphasizes the occasional character of the letters—i.e., since the letters are written to those who had already heard Paul preach, and since the letters discuss specific issues in the churches, the few references to the pre-Easter Jesus are not an index of his importance for Paul's own theology and preaching. Another appeals to Paul's two-week visit with Peter in Jerusalem (Gal. 1:18)—ample time to acquire a body of information about Jesus. This argument has not won widespread support. The third contends that there are numerous allusions to Jesus' teachings in Paul's letters—not quotations or paraphrases, but signs of influence. For instance, Stanley (*Catholic Biblical Quarterly* 23 [1961]) argued that Rom. 13:7 alludes to Matt. 22:21; Rom. 13:8–10 alludes to Jesus' teaching about the great commandment (Mark 12:28–34), Rom. 8:15 to the Lord's Prayer; Rom. 14:14 rests on Matt. 15:11,20 and Rom. 4:4–5 alludes to the parable of the laborers in the vineyard (Matt. 20: 1–16). The more one studies such attempts to locate allusions, the more skeptical one becomes. The first consideration is the most significant. That is, there is no reason to think that Paul mentioned everything he knew about Jesus in letters addressed to specific occasions. Still, it is one thing to affirm, as a hunch, that Paul knew more about Jesus than he says, and another to be able to show it.

On the other hand, it has been argued that in principle Paul was not interested in "the historical Jesus," so that even if he had known more information he would not have used it. This view, advocated already by Schweitzer, was developed especially by Bultmann. Since it has been rather influential, it is useful to examine it more closely. (a) Bultmann rightly saw that Paul's theology is neither an extension nor an elaboration of Jesus' own message.

Paul did not see himself as Jesus' successor. Moreover, a report of Jesus' words and deeds did not constitute the core of Paul's gospel. (b) Paul did not regard Jesus as an example to be followed; indeed, the motif of discipleship is virtually absent from Paul. (c) There is, however, fundamental congruity between Jesus and Paul with regard to the human situation before God. Their vocabulary was different, but what each was expressing existentially was the same. "Jesus says nothing other in his call to repentance than Paul tries to make clear in his theology by means of theoretical argument" ("Jesus and Paul," *Existence and Faith*, p. 188). (d) Yet, there is a difference—Jesus looked forward to the coming of the kingdom but Paul looked back to what had already occurred as the decisive event (cross/resurrection). Still, Bultmann did not account historically for this existential congruity between Jesus and Paul. (e) Later, Bultmann appealed to 2 Cor. 5:16–17 to argue that Paul was not interested in a "fleshly Christ," i.e., the historical Jesus. However, it is almost certain that when Paul wrote of knowing Christ "according to the flesh" the phrase "according to the flesh" modifies the verb not the noun—Paul writes about a way of knowing not about the known.

Bultmann's view expresses a theological position—genuine faith exists only vis-à-vis the word of God, a reality that cannot be investigated as if it were a phenomenon. A "Christ according to the flesh," a "historical Jesus," however, he regarded as precisely such an investigatable phenomenon. Hence Paul, anticipating Bultmann, saw that it would be theologically illegitimate to have included a report of the words and deeds of Jesus in his preaching of the gospel. On the whole, Bultmann is more correct in what he denies —the liberal Protestant concern to make a heroic account of Jesus' words and deeds the core of the gospel—than in what he affirms, namely, that Paul in principle is not interested in the Jesus of history.

The present writer's views can be summarized as follows: (a) It is futile to try to expand the range of the Jesus-traditions known to Paul by looking for allusions. We must try to understand Paul's relation to the Jesus-tradition on another basis. (b) For Paul the words of Jesus were important as church regulations, not as gospel proclamation, kerygma. Even when Paul cites the Jesus-tradition, he does not introduce it as the words of Jesus but as the words of the Lord; that is, through the tradition the living Lord continues to address the church. Paul did not draw as sharp a line between what Jesus once said and what he now says (which is not to say that he obliterated the difference altogether). (c) This means that for Paul what matters is the event as a whole, not individual segments of it, whether incidents or sayings. What is important for Paul is what God did through the event (cross/resurrection), not what Jesus himself had said or done in God's name. To have anchored his theology there would have shifted the whole discussion to another theme—Jesus' own authority. For Paul, however, the cross is not simply an incident, nor an isolable occurrence, but the capstone and epitome of the event as a whole. How Paul understood that event now needs to be brought into view.

THE SHAPE OF THE PIVOTAL EVENT

Paul's understanding of the Christ-event is grasped only when it is perceived in its entirety—that is, when what we call "the historical Jesus" is seen as part of an event that transcends the beginning as well as the end of his life. In other words, the "historical Jesus" is framed by the pre-existence of God's Son and the post-existence of the resurrected one.

It may be useful to pause to reflect on the term "pre-existence" because it is difficult for us to conceive of something being before it exists. Many ancients did not have this difficulty. They believed, just as we do, that "existence" characterized the world of time-space. However, for them this phenomenal, empirical existence of time-space was not the only reality; there was another reality, another "dimension" so to speak. Whereas existence in time-space was real, the other existence was "really real," eternal rather than temporal. In Jewish thought, certain things existed in this super-real existence before they became temporal events—e.g., the name of the Messiah or the Torah. The function of this kind of thinking was to be able to say that important realities in human experience have a transcendent origin, and are not simply the outcome of historical, mundane factors interacting with one another. Thus the

Torah was indeed given through Moses, but the Torah itself is not a historical reality but is as eternal and as transcendent as the mind and will of God. It "was" before it "became." The Jewish theologian, Philo, found Platonic thinking about eternal ideas, of which earthly actualities are copies, congenial to interpret the eternal nature of the Torah. In short, whereas we may need to struggle to think in such terms, many theologians in antiquity took the category "pre-existence" for granted. Paul certainly did, and his letters never justify using it.

The more one believed that God radically transcended the world of time-space, the more important became a mediator, an agent, through whom God created and ordered the world. In Hellenized Judaism, this mediatorial role was played by Sophia, Wisdom. Because Wisdom was understood to be virtually interchangeable with God's will and word, it was easy to infer that God created the world through Wisdom. Two centuries before Paul, the Wisdom of Solomon could celebrate Sophia as the radiation of God himself. She (Sophia is a feminine noun) enters human souls each generation "and makes them friends of God, and prophets" (Wisd. of Sol. 7:27). The word "radiation" (both the process and what is radiated) used of Sophia was later used of the pre-existent Christ by the author of Hebrews; the RSV renders the word as "he reflects the glory of God." In short, what Hebrews 1:1–3a says about the pre-existent Son of God, Hellenized Jewish theology had said previously about Sophia and her relation to the world. The same background shaped Col. 1:15–16.

When NT authors wrote of the pre-existence of Christ, they were applying to him a sophisticated way of thinking which was deeply established in Hellenized Judaism, which in turn was deeply influenced by Greek thought. Paul could assume that he need not explain or justify speaking of an eternal reality which manifested itself in time-space. Because it "was" before it "became," it could be spoken of as *pre*-existing. What early Christians claimed was that this pre-existing reality became Jesus. They did not hold that Jesus pre-existed; rather what pre-existed was God's Son who became Jesus. All incarnational Christology rests on such a conceptual basis.

Apparently it was Hellenistic Jewish Christianity which first developed incarnational Christology. Instead of saying that Jesus was installed into his messianic office at resurrection (as Acts 2:36 states), or instead of saying that he was anointed Son of God at his baptism (as Mark 1:9–11 reports), or instead of saying that Jesus was Son of God from the moment of conception onward, as the Matthean and Lukan stories suggest, incarnational Christology begins prior to the existence of Jesus and regards his life as a stage in the role of the Son of God. The fact that already Paul assumes such a three-stage Christology (pre-existence, existence, post-existence) shows that these modes of thinking about Christ existed side by side almost from the start. It would be another century before these modes would be combined into the orthodox Christology, according to which the incarnation of the pre-existent Son of God occurred at the wondrous conception in Mary's womb. In the NT itself, no one put all of the elements together this way.

Before looking more closely at Paul's understanding of the Christ-event, several general observations are appropriate. (a) There are no passages in the letters designed to instruct the readers in Christology. Christological statements, even the longer ones, always appear where something else is discussed. Although christological issues were deeply involved in Paul's controversies, Christology proper (e.g., appropriate titles for Jesus, incarnation) does not seem to have been the issue. (b) This means that Paul's christological statements do not constitute a peculiarly Pauline Christology; rather, they express a characteristically Pauline interpretation of christological motifs, categories, and titles which were widely shared in Hellenistic gentile and Hellenistic Jewish Christianity. (c) Consequently, Paul's Christology was part of the gospel he proclaimed and taught. Without a Christology he could scarcely have proclaimed his gospel at all. This is why we are discussing Paul's Christology in this context, not in Part Three. (d) Paul appears to have been more interested in the post-existence of Christ than in his pre-existence.

What Paul says about Christ's pre-existence is extremely limited. We already noted the idea that the pre-existent Christ was present with Israel in the wilderness (1 Cor. 10:1–5; see pp. 10, 28). When

Paul called Christ the "wisdom of God" in 1 Cor. 1:24 he assumes that the Corinthians know that the divine Sophia has been reinterpreted as Christ, but he does not discuss the idea. Second century writers like Justin emphasized Christ's role in the OT and in the experience of Israel because they understood the pre-existent Christ as the divine Logos (Word), virtually interchangeable with Sophia. But Paul himself does not develop this possibility in his letters. He may very well have done so in his preaching, however. In 1 Cor. 8:6 he assumes that what was said about Wisdom is true of Christ: "through whom are all things and through whom we exist." How Paul connected the role of the pre-existent Wisdom with the mission of Jesus is not clear; what is clear is that Paul did not regard Jesus as a wise man, or as a teacher of wisdom. Rather, for Paul, he was Wisdom.

What Paul says about the "incarnation" (a word he does not actually use) is rather diverse. Sometimes the subject of the verb is God: "God sent forth his Son, born of woman" (Gal. 4:4; see also Rom. 8:3); this "sending" does not refer to God's sending Jesus forth from the carpenter shop but to his sending the pre-existent one into time-space to become Jesus. Sometimes the subject of the verb is Christ himself, as in 2 Cor. 8:9 (see also Rom. 1:3; Phil. 2:6-7). As with the death of Christ, so the incarnation is spoken of either as an act of God or as an act of God's son.

The most important christological passage is the hymn in Phil. 2:6-11, which Paul uses as a warrant for an ethical injunction (see the context in 2:3-4:12). The hymn itself is not concerned with ethics (the moral example of Jesus) but with the "shape" of the Son's career. No christological passage in Paul's letter has generated more discussion than this one. (Martin's *Carmen Christi* provides the best overview of the issues and the literature.) Only the most important aspects of this passage can be mentioned here. (a) Every translation must supply the verb in verse 5b, and whatever verb is supplied reveals a particular understanding of Paul's point. The RSV's "which you have in Christ Jesus" reveals the longstanding interpretation that the hymn celebrates "the mind of Christ." I prefer something like "which also you think in Christ" or "which also was embodied in Christ." (b) The phrases in

vv. 7–8 mark the successive stages in the humiliation of the pre-existent one: Did not count equality with God a thing to be grasped (the RSV beautifully preserves the ambiguity of the Greek—"to be grasped" can mean either held onto or reached for), emptied himself, taking the form of a servant (or slave), being born (better, coming into existence) in the likeness of man, humbled himself and became obedient unto death. (It is widely believed that Paul inserted "even death on a cross".) (c) The turning point is at v. 9, where the exaltation (by resurrection) is mentioned.

Exegetes disagree over whether the lines that characterize the downward movement of the Son toward death consciously contrast Christ's obedience with Adam's disobedience, just as they disagree over whether "servant" alludes to the Suffering Servant of Isaiah. We should not forget that this is a piece of poetry (though scholars disagree on how to apportion the lines into strophes), not a precise theological analysis; poetry highlights and celebrates, and deliberately sets up resonances with known motifs. Accordingly one must not read too much out of, or into, the passage.

For our immediate concern, it is important to see, first, that had Paul not agreed with this hymn he would not have quoted it. It must accord with what he had preached about Christ to the Philippians. Second, the shape of the incarnation is humiliation, weakness, and obedience—as 2 Cor. 8:9 also implies. Third, implicit in this passage is the view that no one could have looked at Jesus and concluded, "There goes God in the flesh." Not even the principalities and powers recognized him as the Lord of glory, otherwise they would not have had him crucified (1 Cor. 2:8). Fourth, if this passage puts us in touch with how Paul preached Christ, then it is clear that his preaching had no place for the exorcism stories we find in Mark, which report that the demonic powers recognized Jesus' true identity and tried to defend themselves against his power (Mark 1:24). Indeed, it is unlikely that Paul would have found any miracle stories about Jesus congenial to his gospel, for they all expressed the view that Jesus is a bearer of divine power. For Paul, however, the career of Jesus was not marked by power but by weakness and vulnerability, even to the point of death. It is interesting to speculate on what sort of gospel Paul might have written.

What Paul says about the post-existent Son is also quite diverse. For convenience, we can cluster the references into two groups. First, Paul sometimes speaks of the present activity of the post-existent one, now the Lord. Later theologians would have to cope with the ease with which Paul shifts from statements about what Christ is now doing among the believers to what the Spirit is doing (thus according to Rom. 8:34 Christ intercedes for us before God, but in v. 26 it is the Spirit that does this). According to 2 Cor. 3:17 "the Lord is the Spirit." This sentence must not be reversed, because for Paul the Spirit is not Lord but rather the Lord is present through the Spirit and thereby remains sovereign precisely in what we might call "religious experience." Because the Lord is actively at work (in, with, or through the Spirit) among believers, Paul can give his exhortations "in the Lord" (1 Thess. 4:1). The resurrection exalted Jesus and translated him into a state of sovereignty and into a mode of being in which he is intimately related to everyone who believes and has the Spirit.

Second, Christ's own present status is transitional. According to 1 Cor. 15:24, Christ is now conqueror of hostile powers, including death (Rom. 14:9), but when this conquest is complete Christ's own status will change. Thus Paul's understanding of Christ's post-existent work is governed by his expectation of the Lord's return which Paul believed to be imminent. Here too Paul uses a diverse vocabulary. He can call it the *parousia* (coming) of the Son (1 Thess. 1:10), but usually he speaks of the coming of the Lord (1 Thess. 2:19; 3:13; 4:15; 5:23; Phil. 4:5), and once of awaiting a savior from heaven (Phil. 3:20). He can speak of God as the future judge (Rom. 2:16; 3:6), and he can also say that the judge will be Christ (2 Cor. 5:10; see also 1 Cor. 4:5). He can allude to the future coming of the Lord because it was a fixed part of his preaching, as he says in 1 Thess. 1:9–10.

What, then, was the "shape" of the pivotal event in Paul's preaching? The event of Jesus was part of the career of God's Son which began before creation and will end at the parousia, when all things will be transformed and God will be "all in all." The event of Jesus itself was characterized by obedience, vulnerability, and weakness to the point of death, and was followed by exaltation to Lordship now being exercised in God's name until the end. In other words, the event of Jesus derives its significance in part from the fact that it is linked to the OT (Rom. 1:2), and in part from the fact that it is seen in a mythic framework. Paul did not have to invent the framework when he preached the gospel; it was already available in the cultural and religious heritage which he shared with his readers. What was new was the way it was correlated with Jesus, whose historical life ended on the cross but whose eschatological life began at resurrection. What made the event good news was the insight that the cross occurred "for our sins," and that the resurrection of Jesus was the prototype of our own transformation.

Having sketched the gospel which Paul preached, we turn next to explore the redemptive response which Paul elicited from those who believed what he had to say.

CHAPTER FOUR

THE SALVIFIC RESPONSE

In Paul's gospel, the message about Christ was one center of an ellipse; the other center was his hearers. That is, Paul's statements about God and Christ were always worked out vis-à-vis their significance for the human condition. What the gospel announces is not a set of assertions about God and Christ that one can acknowledge as true without having one's life changed. To put it more formally: Christology implies soteriology (the understanding of salvation), and vice versa.

The salvific significance of the Christ-event as proclaimed in the gospel was expressed in various ways by Paul. Each term highlighted a particular facet of the human condition and its appropriate resolution. For example, reconciliation implies that the human condition is alienation or hostility with respect to God; redemption is buying back, as when a person redeems his radio at a pawn shop. Other characteristic word-pictures include justification (being set in right relation), new creation, and adoption. Absent from Paul's vocabulary of salvation were forgiveness and new birth (or regeneration). The most comprehensive term was *sotēria,* salvation.

What Paul's gospel announced was not publicly manifest—that Christ died for our sins and was resurrected by God to be the Lord. Only the crucifixion was a public fact, but its salvific meaning was inseparable from the resurrection. Therefore Paul's message was gospel, good news, only if it was believed. Consequently Paul, like every early Christian preacher, called for faith. Apart from faith, Paul's word brought no salvation. This is why the discussion of the response will consider first Paul's understanding of faith. Because those who believed what Paul said were baptized, the second section will consider Paul's interpretation of Christian baptism.

Finally, we shall look at his understanding of the new community, the church.

FAITH AS TRUST

Faith as a personal decision and commitment was endemic to Christianity from the start, because one became a Christian by believing a message, not by being faithful to inherited religious beliefs and customs. This is why Christians were, and continue to be called "believers." Moreover, in Paul's day, all believers were converts—first generation Christians. None of them had grown up in a Christian community; none became Christian by claiming the faith of the previous generation as his or her own. Furthermore, probably most of them had been "religious" in some sense, whether as members of a synagogue, as worshipers of civic gods, or as initiates of the mystery cults such as Isis and Osiris. Consequently, most persons came into Christianity with other notions about faith, sacraments, religious customs, etc. Paul's understanding of faith, itself rooted in Judaism but reshaped by his experience with the risen Christ, therefore had to maintain its identity and develop its profile in a complex setting which repeatedly threatened to distort it. (Paul's defense of faith and its adequacy is considered in Part Three.)

For Paul faith is a response to a proclamation, a spoken word. Nothing could be farther from Paul than the popular notion that it does not matter so much what a person believes so long as one believes it sincerely enough and believes it fervently enough so that it "works." That makes faith a psychological state; salvation then results from success in believing, in cultivating and maintaining a disposition. That, in turn, would make salvation into an achievement, something attainable by anyone who attained a requisite intensity of faith. There is, of course, such a thing as the dynamics of faith, just as there are patterns and processes (describable psychologically) by which one comes to faith and lives by it, but Paul was not interested in describing them or in reflecting on them. His concern was theological.

Rom. 10:17 is basic, though difficult to translate adequately. The RSV has, "So faith comes from what is heard, and what is heard comes from the preaching of Christ." The NEB has, "faith is awakened by the message, and the message that awakens it comes through the word of Christ." "The preaching of Christ" (RSV) or "the word of Christ" (NEB) does not mean Christ's own preaching; rather, it means the message whose content is Christ. Moreover, both the NEB's "awakened by the message" and the RSV's "faith comes from what is heard" obscure what Paul literally wrote: "faith comes from hearing" (*akoē*). This accent on hearing as the event which awakens faith is central to Paul. It is not reducible to hearing sermons, nor simply equatable with oral communication, though it embraces both.

Three aspects of this "hearing" need to be noted. (a) Faith is a response, not an inference, deduction, or value judgment on a body of information—though it may include these. Neither an inference, nor a deduction, nor a value judgment is good news *for* the self because these processes are acts *of* the self. From Paul's angle, the self that needs salvation can no more generate its own salvation than a psychotic can become his or her own therapist. The self needing salvation must be accosted by a word that offers an alternative and calls for a response. Paul's word for that response is *pistis,* usually translated "faith."

(b) Hearing implies that the gospel must be articulated. A deed of love or compassion can embody it, but a deed remains ambiguous apart from interpretation. For example, Jesus' exorcisms embodied his message, but they were interpreted as evidence that he was in league with the devil (Mark 3:22). Therefore, for Paul the crucifixion was gospel only if it were presented, not as the story of a martyr for a cause, but as God's act, as an event for our sins. Only if the meaning of the Christ-event is articulated for the human dilemma can one respond to it appropriately.

(c) The response that is appropriate to hearing is heeding. Paul himself connected *akoē* (hearing) with *hypakoē* (heeding, obeying), for he understood faith as obedience. When he mentioned the Thessalonians' coming to faith, he wrote of their "obedience" (1 Thess. 1:8); in Rom. 1:8 he wrote of "your faith" and in Rom. 16:19 of "your obedience," clearly meaning the same thing. In Rom. 1:5 he actually used the phrase, "obedience of faith," probably meaning "obedience which is faith," for Rom. 10:16 refers to those who have rejected the gospel as not "obeying" it, not heeding what they heard, not responding with *pistis*. How does one "obey" good news?

When Paul understands faith as obedience, he does not regard the gospel as a command. Rather, it is a message which makes a claim on the hearer, one which calls for a response that has a moral quality to it, not merely an intellectual assent. This moral quality of the response shows that faith is trust, for trust is a moral act. It energizes the will no less than the mind or feelings; trust is a response of the whole self. When that response is to a word that makes a claim on the hearer, that response can be called obedience.

Trust is a useful way of expressing what Paul means by *pistis*. Indeed, the passive verb of the same root word is normally translated "entrusted with" (Rom. 3:2; Gal. 2:7; 1 Thess. 2:4; 1 Tim. 1:11; Titus 1:3). "Trust" is both a verb and a noun, but we have no verbal form for "faith" (we cannot say, "She faiths") but must shift to "believe." But "believe" also creates difficulties, for its opposite is to disbelieve, and sometimes doubt. Moreover, because "believe" is often associated with "beliefs" it is easy to slip into understanding faith primarily as believing beliefs (assenting to doctrines). While *pistis* has a specified object, the primary response Paul sought was not consent to the truth of his statements but rather a personal entrustment of the self to what the gospel announced. To trust is to commit oneself. To trust a person is to rely on that person and to allow oneself to be shaped by that person on a deep level, for the object of trust shapes the truster. To trust a message is to rely on it, to act on it, to be shaped by it. The more radical the message, the deeper the response. In fact, who we are is determined by whom and what we trust (or distrust), by what we count on. Our identity is constituted by the pattern or network of trusts, the configuration of that to which we are committed because we deem it trustworthy. That in which all our trusts are finally grounded is what we call "God," and functions as "God" even if one is not explicitly or constantly "religious."

When Paul called for trust, then, he was calling for reconfiguration of the self. To trust God as presented in the message of the

cross/resurrection and of Jesus' Lordship and coming, is to challenge the previous configurations of trust and their ground. If one
rejects the gospel, one maintains the status quo; if one accepts the
message, one begins to realign that configuration—one heeds the
message, "obeys" the gospel. If the message were a command, a
law, this response might be compliance, not obedience. But for
Paul, the message is a word about what God has done for humanity while it was still enmeshed in false commitments (in sin):
"While we were yet sinners, Christ died for us" (Rom. 5:8). That
is, it is a message about an act of God's grace. The only way one
can heed the news of God's grace is to entrust oneself to this God.

Faith/trust is also confession, deliberate avowal. For Paul, trust
is genuinely Christian only when it is directed toward someone or
something outside the self—God, the gospel, and the Christ it announces. Were this not the case, Paul would have faith in faith;
he would trust the power of trusting. That would make the realign-
ment of trusts depend on the intensity of trust. One would end up
trying to "believe harder"; those who believed best would be most
saved. Moreover, because the gospel is spoken to persons who
already have a network of trusts, it does not reach them as neutrals
but as persons whose lives already embody commitments, tacit or
explicit. To trust the gospel therefore calls for a deliberate decision,
an act of avowal, a confession. Calling Christians "believers" is
really shorthand, for they are not persons who major in believing.
Rather, they are persons who believe what the gospel says and
whom it proclaims, and who entrust themselves to it deliberately.

This intimate relationship between trusting and confessing is
made explicit in Rom. 10:9, where Paul uses traditional language
probably associated with baptism: "If you confess with your lips
that Jesus is Lord and believe in your heart that God raised him
from the dead, you will be saved." This sentence is laced into
a complex interpretation of Deuteronomy 30. Paul's exegetical
method is like that used at Qumran, the so-called midrash-pesher
method. A line of Scripture is quoted, followed by a statement of
its current meaning, "this is. . . ." Deut. 30:14, referring to the
Torah, reads, "The word is near you, in your mouth and in your
heart." Paul says that this is the "word of faith which we preach"

—the message that calls for a self-entrusting response. The carefully balanced sentence shows that Paul is writing about a single act:

| confess | mouth | Jesus is Lord | righteousness |
| believe | heart | resurrection | salvation |

To confess is to acknowledge that the stated content is both true and "true for me." To confess Jesus as Lord is to avow that he has an ultimate claim on my life and that this claim is valid because of what God had done through him. To believe the resurrection with the heart is to believe it with one's will and emotions; it is a matter of commitment and trust.

In the foregoing verse Paul identified that toward which confession and trust are directed as assertions of fact; he used traditional formulations introduced by "that": "that Jesus is Lord," etc. (see also 1 Thess. 4:14). But sometimes Paul also speaks of trust in Christ, and uses a variety of expressions to do so. These are commonly rendered by the same phrase, "faith in Christ." For example, in Phil. 1:29 and Gal. 2:16 Paul writes of believing *eis auton* (toward, unto, *in* him). In Rom. 10:11, using the LXX, he writes of believing *on* him (*ep' autō*). In addition Paul uses *pistis* with the genitive, "of Christ" which at first glance suggests Christ's own faith (see Rom. 3:22,26; Gal. 2:16,20; Phil. 3:9). However, most interpreters regard this genitive as defining the object trusted, and translate it as "faith in Christ." Now another question emerges: What is the relation between trust directed to a statement ("that . . . .") and trust directed toward a person, Christ?

It is easy to overemphasize the difference between the two. For Paul there is no substantial difference between personal trust in Jesus Christ and trust/faith directed toward gospel-statements about God's deed in Christ, for the Christ whom Paul trusts is identical with the Christ announced in the "that. . . ." statements.

Because Paul understood trust to be the sole condition for being rightly related to God, he saw that gentiles need not become Jews in order to be valid Christians. He found support for this in the Scripture itself: "No one who believes in him will be put to shame" (Rom. 10:11, quoting Isa. 28:16). Paul took this at face value: if no one believes in vain, then everyone who believes/trusts is saved. So he continues, "for there is no distinction between Jew and Greek [gentile]; the same Lord is Lord of all and bestows his riches upon all who call upon him [= make the confession], for 'everyone who calls upon the name of the Lord will be saved' " (Rom. 10:12–13, quoting Joel 2:32).

It is useful to note the import of Paul's understanding of trust for his mission. In the first place, if one is rightly related to God by trusting him, then this relation is available to every person as a person, as a self. One does not need to become a Jewish self, or a sophisticated self, or any other kind of self in order to qualify. Rather, it is precisely as a human self that one can trust God on the basis of the gospel. In other words, Paul broke through all categories and divisions which classified people into groups and social strata; he laid hold of the rudimentary, constitutive factor in every self—the network of trusts that makes a self what it is. This is why he could say, "there is neither Jew nor Greek, there is neither slave nor free, there is neither male nor female; for you are all one in Christ" (Gal. 3:28). Of course Paul knew that these distinctions still existed. But they no longer determined who one really is before God, nor decisively modified the right relation to God which is trust. Every self that trusts God on the basis of the gospel is rightly related to its ground.

Second, Paul broke through to the corresponding fundamental meaning of "God." In Rom. 3:29–30, Paul appeals precisely to the core doctrine of Judaism—that "God is one"—to argue that "God is not God of Jews only." Just as there is "neither Jew nor Greek" person before God but only persons, so there is neither "Jewish God" nor "Greek God" who deals with persons. Rather, the one God rectifies the one situation in which all persons find themselves, and does so by means of one relationship—trust. Paul did not achieve this remarkable clarity by asserting the innate goodness of all persons, nor by appealing to the spark of divinity in every self, but by uncovering the solidarity of all persons in bondage to sin. That theme will concern us in Part Three. Right now, however, we will turn to that event which marked the entry of Jew and gentile into a new community, baptism.

BAPTISM INTO CHRIST

How Paul presented baptism in connection with his preaching the gospel is rather elusive. 1 Cor. 1:14–17 implies that he did not make baptism crucial to his mission. Because he nonetheless assumes that his Christian readers have all been baptized, it is clear that baptism was part of Paul's mission. Moreover, Paul repeatedly made baptism the basis on which he built an argument, thereby showing that it was a fundamental component of the response he sought for his preaching. Still, 1 Cor. 1:14–17 shows that Paul did not know the tradition in Matt. 28:16–20, according to which the risen Jesus not only commissioned the apostles to baptize but also specified the formula they were to use.

In order to understand how Paul may have presented baptism to his converts, it is necessary to combine what little we know about early Christian baptism with what we can infer from what Paul assumes in his letters.

Several things can be said about early Christian baptism in Paul's time. (a) Baptism was not invented by Christians nor derived from Jesus' own mission. Yet Christians began baptizing those who accepted their message. It is not known whether they derived this practice from John the Baptist's precedent, or precisely how they interpreted it. (b) Baptism functioned as a rite that marked entry into the Christian community. (c) The rite itself was apparently by immersion. The occasion was marked by an act of confession and administered "in the name of Jesus" (Acts 2:38; 1 Cor. 1:13; the triune formula in Matt. 28:19 was developed later). (d) The problem of whether to baptize infants of Christian parents did not arise in Paul's time. Then, it was those who confessed Jesus as Lord (and their households, according to Acts 16:15) who were baptized. (e) It is highly unlikely that any Christian would have regarded baptism as "only symbol," as an action whose main importance lay in what it signified "outside" the action itself. Rather, for the ancients in general, rites actually did something; the action had power. In other words, it is likely that early Christians regarded baptism as a sacramental act. (f) Early Christians assumed that the gift of the Holy Spirit was linked with baptism, that every baptized person received the Spirit.

We may assume that Paul presented baptism in accordance with these common understandings. However, normally religious rites persist but receive various interpretations. In this light, we can understand why Paul did not emphasize forgiveness of sins but participation in Christ's death. The rite was the same, but the interpretation was relatively new. It appears that this interpretation had not been developed in Palestinian Jewish Christianity. Was it then original with Paul? Apparently not, for he asked the Roman readers who had not yet heard him preach, "Do you not know that all of us who have been baptized into Christ Jesus were baptized into his death?" (Rom. 6:3). He assumes that they—Hellenistic Jewish and Hellenistic gentile Christians—share his view that baptism is "baptism into Christ."

Such an understanding of baptism is possible only if "Christ" is understood in a particular way. In Rom. 5:12–21, Paul had contrasted Adam and Christ, not simply as individuals but also as "corporate persons"—persons who, without losing their individuality, included others. It is exceedingly difficult to conceptualize this because our thinking is profoundly individualistic; the "social contract" view of society and of government allows us to think of isolates deliberately forming aggregates, but inhibits us from thinking of actual participation in a single person "at the head of the line." Something of an analogy may be useful, however. Blacks often sensed that what happened to Martin Luther King was happening to them as well. When he was at the White House, they were there; when he was shot, they were shot. This analogy may be suggestive, but it also has clear limits, for Dr. King was a symbolic representative of the whole. For Paul, however, Christ and Adam were more than representative figures, ones who "stood for" a group. They embodied the group and determined its fundamental character.

Baptism "into Christ" was a rite by which one became a participant in Christ, the inclusive Man (person, not male!), the new Adam (a phrase Paul does not actually use). This participation in Christ was not a "mystical experience" of conscious identification or absorption into Christ. The accent was not on consciousness at all or on "religious experience" but rather on the "objective" transference into a domain of power. To be baptized into Christ is to be included in the domain of Christ, his field of force.

The same understanding lies behind the rather complex passage in Galatians 3, where Paul argues that the promise to Abraham is fulfilled in Christ. Paul notes (Gal. 3:16) that Gen. 12:7 mentions Abraham's "seed" (i.e., offspring), and that the noun is singular. So Paul concludes that Abraham's offspring is Christ. At the end of the chapter Paul says "in Christ Jesus you are all sons of God, through faith" (Gal. 3:26). Because whoever has been baptized into Christ has "put on" Christ, now there is neither Jew nor Greek, slave nor free, male nor female, "for you are all one in Christ Jesus. And if you are Christ's you are Abraham's offspring. . . ." Paul reasons this way because he believes baptism actually makes a person participate in Christ.

Paul shared with Hellenistic Christianity the interpretation of baptism as a rite which made one a participant in Christ, but his own emphasis concerned the center of "Christ"—the cross and resurrection. Paul never says that the baptized participate in Christ's post-existent glory, let alone his divinity. Rather, in keeping with his focus on the cross, he says that those who were baptized were "baptized into his death" (Rom. 6:3). In other words, this phrase specified how "baptism into Christ" is to be understood. Paul's phrase "buried with him through baptism into death" is the heart of the matter. Rom. 6:1–11 is characterized by expressions which we must render as "being X with Christ"—buried with him (v. 4); planted together, i.e., grown together (RSV: united with, v. 5), crucified with (v. 6), die with (v. 8), live with (v. 8). What is in view is not an empathetic act but a sacramental one which actually united the baptizand with Christ. Paul does not mean that baptism somehow makes the past event of Christ present to the individual; it is rather the other way around—the individual is made a participant in Christ's death.

It is important to note that although Paul insists that the baptizand participates in Christ's death, Paul *never* says that one also participates in Christ's resurrection by baptism. Rom. 6:8 reads, "But if we have died with Christ [as indeed we have] we believe that we *shall* also live with him." Participation in Christ's resurrection is future. One reason the Letters to the Colossians and Ephesians are considered to be deutero-Pauline is that they regard participation in Christ's resurrection as something already experienced (Col. 3:1; Eph. 1:20). Rom. 6:4, on the other hand, reads, "we were buried . . . with him . . . so that *as* Christ was raised from the dead . . . we too might walk in newness of life." In short, Christ's resurrection is the basis of a new moral life; the actual resurrection of the Christian awaits the parousia.

Apparently the Corinthian Christians did infer that already they participated also in Christ's resurrection and that this gave them a measure of invulnerability in the world (i.e., they were sacramental enthusiasts). To counter this, Paul compares the post-baptismal Christians with Israel in the wilderness, even saying that the latter had been "baptized into Moses" when they went through the sea; yet they did not reach Canaan because their "post-baptismal sin" was so great that they were destroyed (1 Cor. 10:1–13). Paul's "consider yourselves dead to sin and alive to God in Christ Jesus" (Rom. 6:11) means that the baptized are to claim now the new life of the future resurrection, but to do so as a warrant for a new ethic. This is why Paul's exhortations can be grounded in baptism (see 1 Cor. 6:9–11).

THE NEW COMMUNITY

Just as Paul both shared the early Christian understanding of baptism and developed his own accent, so he shared certain understandings of the church and at the same time contributed his own emphasis—the body of Christ.

The fact that Paul's letters use some traditional terms for the Christian community without explaining them shows that he had already introduced this terminology as part of his teaching. One of these terms is "saints" (Rom. 8:27; 12:13; 15:25,26; 16:2; 1 Cor. 6:1; 16:1; Phil. 1:4; 4:22). Basically "saints" are not particularly holy persons who stand out from the rest by their unusual spirituality. Paul would have repudiated anyone singling him out as "St. Paul," just as he would have refused to call Peter "St. Peter." Every Christian is a saint, a person made holy (sanctified) by the presence of God's holy Spirit. In this light, the RSV's translation of Rom. 1:7 and 1 Cor. 1:2 is misleading if not plainly wrong: "called to be saints." Sainthood is not a goal toward which the believer is invited. Rather, it should be translated "called saints"; Christians are, by definition, "called." "Called saints" does not mean "labelled 'saints' " (as in "the people called 'Methodists' "); rather, "called" refers to God's sovereign act of including these persons in the People of God. ("Saints" is an OT term for the elect people, especially the eschatological People of God.) Paul addressed gentile Christians as "saints" because he regarded them as part of the eschatological People of God, "The Israel of God" (Gal. 6:16).

A second term for the community which was not peculiar to Paul is *ekklēsia,* commonly translated "church." In the LXX *ekklēsia* translates *qahal,* assembly or congregation. For Paul *ekklēsia* usually refers to the local congregation (1 Thess. 1:1), as the plural shows (1 Cor. 11:16; Gal. 1:2; 2 Cor. 8:1). However, it can also be used of the Christian community as a whole, for when 1 Cor. 12:28 says "God has appointed in the church first apostles," etc., Paul clearly has more in view than the Corinthian congregation. (See also 1 Cor. 15:9.)

Paul's understanding of the church manifests itself throughout his letters; indeed, one can say that his entire letter-writing activity is his struggle for a right understanding of what it means for Christians to be church. This is apparent not only in his rather stringent discipline (e.g., 1 Cor. 5:1–6:11), but also in his concern for the moral life of Christians (e.g., Romans 12–13), for order in worship (1 Corinthians 12–14), and for internal harmony (Phil. 2: 1–4; 4:2–3). What enhances the community ("builds up," "edifies") is prominent in the warrants Paul adduces for his moral appeals (e.g., 1 Cor. 14:2–4; 1 Thess. 5:11).

On the other hand, Paul's letters show only slight interest in providing the readers with a correct doctrine of the church, an ecclesiology; nor do they show any concern for questions of church polity (proper organization). Rather, in Paul's small house church congregations diverse roles were regarded as manifestations of the diverse gifts of the Spirit, as 1 Corinthians 12 shows. This fluidity in leadership roles is one of the things that distinguished Paul's own understanding of the church from what the author of Ephesians wrote in Paul's name. In Eph. 4:7-12, the writer regards distinct offices of the church as gifts of the Spirit, whereas Paul wrote of roles and capacities to function in particular ways (1 Cor. 12:4-11). Moreover, in Ephesians the church itself has become the subject-matter of theological reflection—in fact, the church is now God's destined answer to the problem of the cosmos because it is the body of Christ.

"Body of Christ" may well have been Paul's own distinctive contribution to the community's self-understanding. Ephesians and Colossians developed this beyond Paul; the undisputed letters never *describe* the church as the body of Christ in so many words (as does Eph. 1:22f.; Col. 1:18). Instead Paul *addresses* the readers, "you are the body of Christ" (1 Cor. 12:27), and he does so as a warrant for an exhortation to unity.

The metaphor of a body with diverse organs was known also in popular Stoicism. In this vein Paul *compares* the church with a body in 1 Cor. 12:12-26. But when he *identifies* the readers as the body of Christ (1 Cor. 12:27) he moves beyond metaphor toward myth—the myth of a cosmic body constituted by Christians. The extent to which this identification reflects a gnostic myth of the cosmic redeemer, whose body consists of the saved, is disputed. Barrett (*The First Epistle to the Corinthians,* ad loc.), for instance, says that the genitive is "not of identity but of possession"—not the body which is Christ but the body that belongs to Christ. Yet 1 Cor. 12:13 writes of being "baptized into one body," suggesting that somehow the body of Christ is a transcendent entity, not simply an earthly community. In the last analysis, it is less than clear exactly how Paul thought of "the body of Christ."

Paul's understanding of the Christian community is disclosed not only in what he said about it and to it, but also in what he said about its rites. We have already commented on baptism; now we turn to the Lord's Supper.

Probably this was the high-point of worship; it is equally probable that this occurred on Sundays (1 Cor. 16:1). Moreover, the Lord's Supper was not separated from the church supper. This separation actually began with Paul's advice to the Corinthians

(1 Cor. 11:17–34, esp. v. 34). The fact that the Lord's Supper was part of the church supper was one of the things that made the crisis in Antioch so severe, for when Jewish Christians withdrew from the common table they also withdrew from the communion table (Gal. 2:11–13).

How Paul interpreted the Lord's Supper when he introduced it to his churches must be inferred from the tradition which he taught (1 Cor. 11:23–25) and from 1 Cor. 10:16–17 where he reminds them of what the meal means in order to make another point.

The Lord's Supper tradition in 1 Corinthians 11 is the oldest written form of the tradition, antedating Mark by fifteen or more years; yet Mark's form of the tradition (Mark 12:22–25) is often regarded as essentially older, less Hellenistic, than Paul's (probably developed at Antioch). Two features call for a comment. (a) The Lord's Supper tradition celebrates what the other piece of tradition reports—that "Christ died for our sins" (1 Cor. 15:3). This manifests itself in the phrasing. Not only does the tradition begin with "on the night when he was handed over" (see p. 36), but the language makes more explicit what is implied in Mark:

Mark: This is my body.
Paul: This is my body which is for you (some MSS: broken for you).
Mark: This is my blood of the covenant (some MSS: new covenant) which is poured out for many.
Paul: This is the new covenant in my blood.

Thus Paul's tradition explicitly extends the atonement theme to the bread. Paul's tradition also recasts the covenant motif in order to make explicit the claim that Jer. 31:31 is now a reality. (b) Paul's tradition includes the command to repeat the rite "in remembrance" of Christ, a motif absent from Mark. This remembrance is more than recollection; it has to do with commemoration, an act in which the meaning of the past is made present. It does not suggest that Christ's death is repeated ritually.

1 Cor. 10:16–17 gives us the word "communion" for the Supper. Here Paul reminds the Corinthians that the cup and the bread (the reversed sequence does not reveal a different tradition) are

"communion" (*koinonia*) in the blood of Christ. By drinking and eating the congregation shares in Christ. Because the Corinthians understand this, Paul could appeal: You cannot eat the Lord's Supper and participate in a sacred meal at local shrines as well because this ritual eating makes one a participant in the reality being celebrated (1 Cor. 10:20–21).

It was just this understanding of sacral and sacramental eating/drinking which led to a development which Paul regarded as gross distortion. Precisely what was going on and what the Corinthians thought they were doing continues to be debated. Nonetheless, it is reasonably clear that they understood the Supper in a highly sacramental way. To imagine what was going on, we must recall that the group met in a home of a wealthier Christian whose dwelling could accommodate the group. Moreover, since there was neither a "legal Sunday" nor a standard quitting time from work, there was probably no fixed "church hour" either. People came when they could, and the gatherings may well have lasted for hours, perhaps far into the night (if Acts 20:7 is a clue). Apparently those who arrived first began eating and drinking, so that by the time everyone had arrived, some had already had too much (1 Cor. 11:21). Moreover, the poor were humiliated by the little they brought (v. 22). The Corinthians saw no reason to share with each other or to wait for one another because they understood the religious meaning of eating and drinking as participation in the Lord, apparently emphasizing participation in the risen Lord's power and Spirit. The communing was between the individual and the Lord; what difference did it make who else was or was not there?

Paul does not hesitate to say, "When you meet together, it is not the Lord's Supper that you eat." They certainly thought it was! How then can Paul make such a statement? Because, first, this participation is not primarily in the power and glory of the risen Lord but in his death. This is why he repeats the tradition, and adds his comment: "For as often as you eat this bread and drink this cup, you proclaim the Lord's death until he comes." Second, he goes on to write about "discerning the Lord's body" (1 Cor. 11:29). When he adds that sickness (and even death) has befallen those who participated "unworthily" he shows that he too regards the meal as a sacrament with power which, if abused, brings a curse instead of a blessing. At the same time, the entire context shows that the body of Christ which is to be "discerned" in the occasion is not merely the bread, but also the church. One may even infer that for Paul the body of Christ is not only *on* the table but also *at* the table. This is supported by the fact that 1 Cor. 10: 16–17 explicitly connects the two: "the bread which we break, is it not a participation in the body of Christ? Because there is one loaf, we who are many are one body, for we all partake of the same loaf."

Thus Paul understands the Supper as a sacramental rite which involves the believers not only with Christ, specifically with his death, but also with one another. The unity of the community is not the result of mutual accommodation, a social contract, but the result of being "baptized into one body" and of eating one loaf. Therefore, "if one member suffers, all suffer together; if one member is honored, all rejoice together" (1 Cor. 12:26). What was happening in Corinth was just the opposite. Therefore their meals were not "the Lord's Supper," regardless of how the Corinthians may have understood it and irrespective of how "meaningful" their experiences might have been.

CHAPTER FIVE

THE DEEPER LOGIC OF PAUL'S GOSPEL

The interpreter of Paul meets not only specific concepts, such as grace, law, or Spirit, but also a way of thinking which may seem strange. Grasping Paul's thought therefore requires more than clarifying a group of concepts; it calls also for understanding the perspective within which these concepts function, the deeper logic that gives coherence to this thought.

Because Paul's letters are not treatises in theology but pastoral letters occasioned by particular problems, he did not identify his governing assumptions; nor did he usually indicate the logical connections between them. Ascertaining the deeper coherence of this thought therefore entails certain risks. One may unwittingly impose one's own sense of coherence on Paul; one may also end up making Paul more systematic than he really was. Nonetheless, the risk is worth taking.

In getting at the deeper logic of his gospel, we will focus on three motifs or perspectives rather than on "doctrines": the sovereign freedom of God, creation and new creation, and participation and anticipation. We are not interested here in detecting the origin of these motifs, or in calling attention to the mythic factor in them, but in perceiving their inner theological coherence. Gaining some clarity here will help us understand how Paul deepened certain theological emphases in his letters (Part Three).

THE SOVEREIGN FREEDOM OF GOD

Fundamental to Paul's understanding and interpretation of God is the conviction that God's activity manifests his sovereign freedom to be faithful to himself and to his commitments. This understanding of God was deeply rooted in the OT and in Judaism. Nonetheless, the gospel which Paul preached induced him to rethink this motif and to express it, especially in Romans, in several characteristically Pauline ways. As already noted, it is likely that his own experience of being transformed from a persecutor into a propagator of the gospel radicalized his inherited understanding of God's sovereign freedom. Implicit in his conversion is the radical freedom of God vis-à-vis Paul's life, for his conversion implied that God was not bound to the way Paul was thinking of God or relating to him. Rather, God intervened in his life despite Paul. The logic of this experience implies that a God who is not free to do this cannot do anything decisive about the human situation; conversely, a God who has done this is disclosed as a radically free sovereign committed to setting things right. A God who is not free is reduced to a logarithmic function of culture, of nature's processes, or to the invisible coefficient of human achievement or consciousness. Such a God no longer stands over against culture or humanity with an identity of his own, but is reduced to the guarantee and ground of what is.

It is convenient to probe this motif by considering two polarities: first, intentionality and achievement; second, newness and constancy. Although it was polemical and apologetic situations that elicited Paul's discussions of these themes, they were so fundamental to his gospel that it is appropriate to deal with them here.

Intentionality and Achievement

It is axiomatic for Paul that God has an intent, a will, a goal. Paul's understanding of God is telic (with a view toward the *telos,* end). For Paul, God is not a passive reality, but an intensely active one. Nor is Paul's God a remote divine watch-maker of the 18th century Deists, the Creator who retired after constructing a law-abiding universe. Rather, Paul assumed that God is actively at work in pursuit of his goals. As we shall see, that goal embraces the redemption of creation. At the same time, Paul's letters contain no description of that goal. Nonetheless, his theology is more oriented toward the future than the past, more toward destiny than toward origins. This is because Paul understands himself to be living at the hinge of history, at the dawn of the new age (see below).

Though Paul's thinking embraces all creation, his letters contain remarkably little about his "world-view." Paul does not try to stand outside the world in order to see it as a whole. Rather, he locates himself in a particular place and lifts his eyes to the widest horizon from where he stands, namely, in the vortex where the gospel encountered him as a devout Jew. When Paul thinks about God's purpose he inevitably thinks in terms of Jews and gentiles (to be discussed later), and of Israel's role in God's purpose. He does not think abstractly about humanity (for which he has no word), nor about the self (he says virtually nothing about the nature of the soul).

As a matter of fact, Paul says very little about Israel's vocation in light of God's intentionality. What he does say in Rom. 2:17–29 does not celebrate the Jews' vocation but is actually an indictment of them. He picks up the catchwords of Jewish self-understanding (as he perceives it): "a guide to the blind, a light to those who are in darkness, a corrector of the foolish, a teacher of children, having in the law the embodiment of knowledge and truth." But he juxtaposes this with a list of accusations in order to conclude, " 'the name of God is blasphemed among the Gentiles because of you' " (quoting Isa. 52:5). Nonetheless, the prerogatives of the Jews vis-à-vis the gentiles are affirmed: "they are Israelites, and to them belong the sonship, the glory, the covenants, the giving of the law, the worship, and the promises; to them belong the patriarchs and of their race, according to the flesh, is the Christ" (Rom. 9:4–5).

At this point it is appropriate to ask how Paul understands salvation history in light of the intentionality of God. The term "salvation history" has a checkered history in 19th and 20th century theology. After World War II, Cullmann's book *Christ and Time* made it prominent especially in those Protestant circles unwilling to follow Bultmann's existentialist interpretation; subsequently it became prominent also in Catholic theology, partly because it introduced a dynamic element into biblical theology and thereby freed the Bible from being used primarily to provide proof texts for dogmatics. It was OT study, of course, which evoked the theme in the first place because there was an emerging awareness that the history of Israel as reconstructed by critical historiography differed significantly from the way the OT itself told the story.

Salvation history is one translation of *Heilsgeschichte,* sometimes rendered as "history of salvation": the view that the bulk of the OT (apart from the Wisdom material) regards the individual stories, events, and epochs as "the line of God's action in the events of world history, which leads to the achievement of his purpose of the salvation of mankind" (Richardson, *IDB* 4, p. 171). "Salvation history" has made it possible for interpreters to do several things: (a) to give a green light to critical historiography concerning the individual items in the overall story; (b) to discern a theological unity in the diverse material; (c) to relate the OT to the NT. Thus Richardson continues: "it was by a particular series of historical events, through a particular national history, that God's saving purpose in Jesus Christ was fulfilled. It is because salvation is in the name of Jesus . . . that the biblical history is 'salvation history'; and it is for this reason that the salvation story is the story of Abraham . . . Moses . . . Rahab the harlot . . . David . . . and the prophets . . . and not the story of Buddha, Confucius, Socrates, Mohammed, Rousseau. . . ." (ibid.). Pervading all the variations of salvation history is the view that the OT is a saga of God's dealing with Israel, leading up to Christ—at least in the Christian view of things.

Paul was often called as a chief witness on behalf of this theology. He certainly believed that God's intent came to decisive fulfillment in Christ. But can we say that he understood God's intent in terms of salvation *history*? Hardly! Unless we immediately add that he radically transformed the idea the way he (and his predecessors) transformed "Messiah" into Christ—i.e., the office of a national redeemer-liberator was made into a personal name. True, the sample of Paul's preaching to the Hellenistic synagogue in Acts 13:16–41 does have Paul express a salvation history theology. It begins with the patriarchs, then mentions Exodus (omitting Sinai!), the conquest of Canaan, and highlights of the history up to David; then it moves to John the Baptist and the Jesus-story. But Paul's letters give no indication that he actually preached this way. He did not read the Bible as a holy history; rather, in Rom. 3:2 he calls it "the oracles of God." To be sure, he appeals to some of the events mentioned in Acts 13, but he never discusses them as a sequence which constitutes a salvation history. For Paul the intentionality of God does not work itself out through Israel's history which culminates in Christ. The Christ-event, instead of being the capstone of a development, is a lens through which Paul sees the intent of God in a particular way.

The main place where Paul's understanding differs from that of salvation history is Romans 4, where he interprets Abraham. Paul adduces Abraham in support of his contention in Rom. 3:30—that since God is one, "he will justify the circumcised on the ground of their faith and the uncircumcised because of their faith." For both groups the right relation to God depends on the same thing—sheer trust.

Paul knows that God pronounced Abraham to be righteous in Gen. 15:6, and that the story of Abraham's circumcision is found in Genesis 17. Therefore God's gift of righteousness did not depend on circumcision. Hence circumcision was "a sign or seal of the righteousness which he had by faith when he was still uncircumcised" (v. 11). That is its meaning for Abraham; another meaning has to do with God's purpose. In Rom. 4:17 Paul appeals to Genesis 17, where God renewed the promise before Abraham circumcised himself. The promise includes the statement, "I have made you the father of many nations." With his eye on this statement, Paul asserts that the purpose of Abraham's circumcision was to make him (a) "the father of all who believe *without* being circumcised and who thus have righteousness reckoned to them" on the basis of faith, and likewise (b) "the father of the circumcised who are not merely circumcised but also follow the example of the faith which our father Abraham had *before* he was circumcised" (vv. 11–12). Thus Abraham is the father of all those whose relation to God is a matter of trust; Paul implicitly denies that Abraham is the father of all circumcised Jews, for he is truly father only of those who live by trust.

In Rom. 4:17b–22 Paul returns to Genesis 15 and interprets Abraham's faith as sheer trust in the face of the evidence (i.e., lack of evidence): he and Sarah were too old to have a child. Of Abraham Paul writes, "No distrust made him waver concerning the promise of God, but he grew strong in his faith as he gave glory to

God, fully convinced that God was able to do what he had promised. That is why his faith 'was reckoned to him as righteousness' " (Gen. 15:6). Why be concerned about Abraham's faith? Because what was said of him was "written not for his sake alone but for ours also"; what God did in his case he will do in the case of Christians also: trust "will be reckoned to us who believe in him that raised from the dead Jesus our Lord. . . ." In other words, whoever believes the gospel repeats Abraham's faith (v. 12) because Abraham too believed in the God "who gives life to the dead [an allusion to the deadness of Abraham's virility and of Sarah's fecundity] and calls into existence the things that do not exist" (v. 17). The believers do not believe like Abraham (as v. 12 might imply); rather they "share the faith of Abraham" (v. 16). This means that Christian trust and Abrahamic trust are congruent; the structure of his trust in God is identical with Christian trust in God. The trust of the Christian recapitulates the trust of Abraham, the prototype of everyone who is justified by faith.

Whatever one might think of Paul's exegesis, one thing at least should be clear—he does not see the relation between the gospel and Abraham as one of salvation *history,* for the gospel is not the culmination of what was begun in Abraham but a recovery of it and actualization of it. As Paul said in Gal. 3:8–9, "Scripture, foreseeing that God would justify the Gentiles by faith, preached the gospel beforehand to Abraham, saying 'In thee shall all the nations be blessed' " (Gen. 12:3). Consequently, those who believe "are blessed with Abraham who had faith." God's intent for Abraham is not achieved in the history of Israel but in the existence of a community of Jews and gentiles whose trust in God is Abrahamic.

Having looked at how Paul understands God's intentionality, we turn now to the other aspect of this first polarity, achievement. How does the sovereign freedom of God to achieve his intent manifest itself? One can argue that God achieves his intent for the gentiles when they become Abraham's children by sheer trust; but how can one say that God's intent for Jews is being fulfilled when most Jews were in fact rejecting the gospel? What can Paul say about the frustration of God's intention?

Two possibilities are excluded—(a) God responds by rejecting his people (Rom. 11:1); (b) God's word has "failed" (Rom. 9:6; NEB: has proved false). In rejecting the latter possibility Paul manifests how he understands the sovereign freedom of God. In other words, what is commonly regarded as Paul's doctrine of election and predestination is really his exposition of God's sovereign freedom to achieve his purpose ultimately (Romans 9–11). It will repay us to look more closely at these chapters.

Paul's premise is that "the gifts and the call of God are irrevocable" (Rom. 11:29)—that is, God can be counted on to keep his word, to attain his goal. Were this not the case, God would have neither sovereignty nor freedom vis-à-vis human responses but be at their mercy. At the same time, Paul does not see God as a tyrant who forces his will on his subjects. After all, God's intent is human trust, not mere compliance.

Paul's discussion moves in several steps. First, he argues that the sovereign freedom of God means that God's dealing with his people has never depended on human merit (or achievement), for that would make his relation to Israel a matter of reward, compensation. Right from the start, God determined that Abraham's lineage would run through Isaac, not Ishmael (Rom. 9:6–8), because Isaac's birth was a matter of God keeping his promise. Subsequently, before Isaac's and Rebekkah's twins were born, Jacob was the chosen one. Clearly the choice did not depend on how the boys turned out.

Second, Paul raises objections (using *diatribē* style): Is God unfair? No, because Exod. 33:19 says that God would have mercy on whomever he will. Mercy, by definition, is not something that can be judged to be fair or unfair. Conversely, God's "hardening" Pharaoh's heart shows the same thing: God is free to achieve his purpose as he wills (Rom. 9:14–18). Now comes a double objection: If that is the case, why does God hold persons accountable for their actions ("Why does he still find fault?"), and, "Who can resist his will?" (i.e., Isn't God then a tyrant?). Paul declares these questions to be out of bounds because a creature cannot ask the Creator to justify himself any more than a pot can ask the potter, "Why did you make me this way?" Paul then infers that God has put up with resistance from one group (the unbelieving

Jews) in order to attain his purpose for the others (the gentiles and believing Jews; Rom. 9:19–24). Paul sees that through the gospel "the Gentiles who did not pursue righteousness attained . . . righteousness through faith" but Jews who did pursue righteousness by trying to obey the law failed to reach this righteousness because they rejected the gospel (Rom. 9:25–33, supported by quotations from Scripture). Chapter 10, after restating Paul's gospel, ends with a series of quotations from Scripture which Paul believes interpret the present situation: "I [God] have been found by those who did not seek me" (the gentiles) but God has extended his welcome continually "to a disobedient and contrary people." Still, God has not rejected his people across the board, for Paul himself is proof to the contrary (11:1–2).

The fact that he and other Jewish Christians are a minority is nothing new, for already in Elijah's time there was but a remnant who did not succumb to Baalism. "So too at the present time there is a remnant, chosen by grace" (11:5). Structurally, the theological situation has not changed. In the process of achieving his ends, God has always had to cope with recalcitrant persons. Moreover, God's grace has never been anything but sheer grace, never a mere generous response to human achievement.

Third, Paul sees that through the Jews' rejection of the gospel, salvation has in fact come to gentiles (Rom. 11:11). Paul is reflecting on a historical fact: when Romans was being written, the church was rapidly becoming predominantly gentile, and it may well have seemed to Paul that the rejection of the gospel by Jews and its acceptance by gentiles were related in God's providence. As in Pharaoh's time, so now God uses the "hardening" of one to achieve his purpose with the other: "a hardening has come upon part of Israel until the full number of the Gentiles come in, and so all Israel will be saved" (Rom. 11:25–26). Paul never speculates on how this will happen. Had he done so he would have violated precisely the sovereign freedom of God, for knowing the "how" would imply that God could be manipulated, that the process could be hastened or slowed, that the achievement of God's intent was in human hands after all. (Paul's statement that he increases his ministry to gentiles in order to make Jews jealous and so save some of them should not be taken as a strategy; see Rom. 11:13–14.) But if Paul's trust in God is truly Abrahamic, then Paul must trust God to keep his word with regard to all Israel just as Abraham trusted him to keep his word with regard to the birth of Isaac.

Two things at least should be clear. One, although Romans 9–11 has been the main quarry from which stones for the Christian doctrine of predestination have been cut, Paul's own agenda is quite different. He was not at all interested in explaining which individual would be saved and which not. He was reflecting on the mysterious ways in which things work out in history, on the fact that things turn into opposites (Israel should have said Yes but said No, while gentiles said Yes; the No of the one produced the Yes of the other), and on the fact that neither the Yes nor the No is the last word. This is why in 11:17–21 he warns gentile Christians not to become proud. The sovereign freedom of God is just that—God's innate capacity to achieve his ends without coercion. Two, the deeper logic of Paul's discussion of Jews and gentiles is identical with the logic underlying his discussion of justification by faith. Only if God has sovereign freedom can he make right the relation between himself and the sinner, and do so on his own terms.

Newness and Constancy

The other polarity which makes clear how Paul understood the sovereign freedom of God is newness and constancy; specifically, the radical newness of the gospel and God's constancy. Can Paul affirm both? Or did his zeal for the gospel induce him to conclude that in Christ God had changed the rules? There is no doubt that Paul would have repudiated Marcion, as well as all forms of Marcionism still lurking in many Christian circles—that the OT God is one of law and wrath, but the God of the NT is one of gospel and grace. But then, how did Paul hold together the newness of the gospel and the constancy of God?

The problem of God's constancy is really a problem of the law. If God's purpose has been a right relation to himself based on sheer trust, why did God give the law in the first place? In Galatians 3 Paul wrestles with this question.

Although certain details of the Galatian crisis continue to elude scholarly sleuths, the main point is clear enough: the gentile Galatian Christians were being persuaded that if they wanted to be first-class Christians they must accept circumcision. Thereby they would perfect their present, second-class status into which Paul's gospel had brought them. (The RSV obscures this by translating Gal. 3:3 as "are you now ending with the flesh?"; the NEB is better: "do you now look to the material to make you perfect?") The way Paul appeals to Abraham suggests that his opponents themselves had been appealing to Abraham, perhaps arguing that Abraham was circumcised *after* he was pronounced righteous by God—accordingly, circumcision follows faith as its perfecting sacrament. Apparently the Galatians did not understand that accepting circumcision implied accepting the obligation to observe the law, for Paul writes, "I testify again to every man who receives circumcision that he is bound to keep the whole law" (Gal. 5:2). Yet Christ has redeemed us from this obligation.

Then why did God give the law at all, especially after declaring Abraham to be righteous apart from the law? Did God change the rules? Does not what comes later supersede what preceded? Not at all, he argues, because a ratified will is not changeable (Gal. 3:15). That is, what God promised to Abraham's offspring cannot be claimed by anyone else. And who is Abraham's offspring? Christ! Moreover, those baptized into Christ are Abraham's offspring (v. 16, 29; see pp. 38, 58). In other words, the law given later to Moses "does not annul a covenant previously ratified by God" (v. 17). Were that the case, then God would change the rules of the game. But why then was the law given? "It was added because of transgressions"—that is, sin made the law necessary to restrain humanity, not to produce true life. Judaism's claim that obedience to the law, God's will, leads to life misunderstands the capacity of the law, "for if a law had been given which *could* make alive, then righteousness would indeed be by the law" (Gal. 3:21). The law's failure is discussed in chapter 8.

The function of the law (as something that deals with transgressions) is only temporary, for it was added "till the offspring should come to whom the promise had been made" (Gal. 3:19b)

—that is, until Christ (and those in him). During that period (from Moses to Christ) "the law was our custodian" (better, our warden, or trustee who has charge for a time). But now that the Christ-event has occurred, "now that faith has come," we are no longer under the law. In Gal. 4:1–2 Paul paraphrases his point: a minor, though heir of the estate, "is under guardians and trustees until the date set by the father." But now that the pre-set time has come, the minor is no longer under the guardian but enjoys full rights of the son. And how do we know we are "sons"? Because the Holy Spirit in our hearts prompts us to call God "Abba!" (Papa). Through Christ God himself has terminated the time when the law was in charge, and God has confirmed this through the Spirit. If this be true, then the law is not opposed to God's promises categorically; the God of the gospel is not pitted against the God of the law, because God himself "added" the law for a specific purpose and terminated its role at the set time.

Thus Paul argued that the way of the law was temporary and that its end was foreseen by God from the start. As he said in Gal. 3:8, God himself preached the gospel to Abraham. Anyone who wants to be truly Abrahamic now lives by sheer trust in God, not by law. Thus God's sovereignty manifests itself not in God's freedom to change the rules when he wants to but in keeping his word, in being faithful to himself.

The newness of the gospel does not reflect a U-turn in God's intent but a new time. Now the era of law is superseded because God's intent is being realized, inasmuch as Christ marks the time of fulfillment. Christ is the end (*telos*) of the law (Rom. 10:4). In Rom. 3:21–26 Paul characterizes the redemption in Christ, the *hilastērion* (see p. 35), as occurring to "show God's righteousness, because in his divine forebearance he had passed over former sins"; that is, God ratifies his previous forgiveness of sins. Paul appears to imply that precisely because the law could not give real life, a sacrificial system (epitomized by *hilastērion*) to mediate God's forgiveness was needed. That God "passed over" sins before shows that God did not decide to be gracious on Good Friday. Hence Paul can assert that the gospel does not overturn the law but actually confirms what the law means (Rom. 3:28–31).

CREATION AND NEW CREATION

Being rooted in Judaism and its Scripture, Paul assumed that God is the Creator. Rom. 4:17 refers to God as the one "who calls into existence the things that do not exist," as close to a statement of *creatio ex nihilo* as the NT contains. In Rom. 1:18–20 Paul appropriated the prevalent Hellenistic cosmological argument for the existence of God, namely, that the Creator can be inferred from the creation. But Paul transformed this motif, first by saying that what can be known of God is manifest because God has manifested it (rather than because human minds deduced it); second, this knowledge of God makes persons "without excuse." It does not secure their understanding of God.

Whereas the deutero-Pauline letters to the Colossians and Ephesians emphasize the relation of the pre-existent Son of God to creation (see chapter 3), the undisputed letters virtually ignore this. However, given Paul's appropriation of Jewish wisdom theology, and given the occasional nature of the letters as well, one should not infer that this theme was of no interest to Paul.

What Paul does speak of repeatedly, however, is the host of malign invisible powers which now tyrannize creation. Again, the letters do not provide instruction about them, but assume that "everybody" knew what they were. The fluidity of Paul's terminology shows that he was not concerned to be precise at this point. In Rom. 8:38 he mentions angels, principalities (*archai*), and powers along with other threats to human life. In 1 Cor. 15:24 he writes of rule, authority, and power; Gal. 4:3,9 has *stoicheia,* which RSV and NEB translate "elemental spirits of the universe." Doubtless Paul alludes to the same cluster of invisible powers which Eph. 1:21 calls rule, authority, power, and dominion, and which Eph. 3:10 calls "the principalities and powers in the heavenly places." Paul does not say that the Christian fights "against the principalities, against the world rulers of this present darkness, against the spiritual hosts of wickedness in the heavenly places" (Eph. 6:12), nor that these powers, "whether thrones or dominions or principalities and authorities," were created through the pre-existent Christ (Col. 1:16), though he may well have believed it. Paul never traces the human dilemma or the origin of sin to these powers; nor does he explain how they are related to "the god of this aeon" who blinds unbelievers to the truth of the gospel (2 Cor. 4:4); nor does he blame this "god" for the Jews' rejection of the gospel. Elusive as Paul's thought about these forces is, there is no doubt that he understood the universe to be influenced by them.

More important to Paul was the view that there were two aeons: "this aeon and the aeon to come." Although Paul never uses the entire phrase, his references to "this aeon" show that he assumes the duality (Rom. 12:2; 1 Cor. 1:20; 2:6,8; 3:18; 2 Cor. 4:4; "the present evil age" in Gal. 1:4 is a paraphrase). "Aeon" is not simply epoch; it is a way of characterizing the present world order as a whole. This way of speaking is rooted in Jewish apocalyptic which (a) saw all of history as a whole over against God's pledged redemption, yet (b) did not see any evolution or development from one to the other but regarded the new world order as God's radical alternative to the present. Apparently Paul believed that this change would occur in conjunction with the coming of Christ, the parousia; but his letters show no interest at all in explaining that transformation. Though he says that "the form of this world (*kosmos* here=*aeon*) is passing away" (1 Cor. 7:31), he never describes the age to come.

In Rom. 8:19–23 Paul writes about the redemption of creation from "futility" (NEB: frustration) and from "bondage to decay" (NEB: shackles of mortality)—evidently alluding to the "curse" which befell creation as a result of Adam's sin. Here Paul also says that creation waits eagerly "for the revealing of the sons of God"— i.e., for the full transformation of the Christian self, including the redemption of the body (see chapter 7). This will occur because "the creation itself will be set free from bondage to decay and obtain the glorious liberty of the children of God." This remarkable statement implies solidarity between persons and the created world, so that the redemption of the body—a piece of creation—carries with it the redemption of the whole creation. For Paul there is no such thing as a redemption which separates the self from the creation.

The importance of this theme for Paul was rediscovered by

Käsemann who saw that for Paul God's act in Christ intends to reclaim and reconstitute creation. Seeing this element in Paul's theological horizon helps us understand what he meant by calling Christians "new creation" (2 Cor. 5:17; Gal. 6:15). For Paul the new life in Christ is a harbinger of the redemption of creation. Therefore whoever is in Christ is "new creation."

PARTICIPATION AND ANTICIPATION

Participation and anticipation refer to two modes of thinking about salvation. The discussion of baptism and Lord's Supper (chapter 4) has already shown that for Paul the Christian participates in Christ. What needs to be done at this point is to reflect on the rationale of participation-language. Anticipation, on the other hand, is a basic Pauline way of thinking eschatologically about salvation. Grasping both modes of thought will make it easier to follow Paul as he clarifies certain theological issues (Part Three).

Tannehill identified what is important about participation: "Christ's death and resurrection are not merely events which produce benefits for the believer, but also are events in which the believer himself partakes" (*Dying and Rising with Christ,* p. 1). The Christ-event does not remain external to the believer; nor does the gospel report only something decisive that occurred elsewhere (in Palestine) once upon a time (even if only two decades had elapsed when Paul reached Corinth). An event related externally to the self must be claimed by an act of will; the self repeatedly decides to make the past, distant event relevant by imitating it, by becoming a disciple of the figure. If the figure and his teachings are internalized, this process depends on the discipline and the disposition of the self. Moreover, internalizing an external event requires knowledge of the past, the Jesus-traditions. Finally, this normative tradition gauges whether the internalization is inadequate or inappropriate.

These somewhat abstract formulations actually describe Matthew's view of the relation between the believer and the Christ-event. For Matthew, the Christian is a disciple who is summoned to shape his or her life on the pattern of Jesus (Matt. 28:20).

Making the Christian confession, "Jesus is Lord" does not save, but doing God's will embodied in Jesus (Matt. 7:21–23). The most serious charge against the disciple, as against the Pharisees, is hypocrisy—the manifest gap between professing and performing. There is nothing in Matthew that corresponds to Paul's baptism into Christ, to participation in Christ, nor to Paul's emphasis on the Spirit who indwells the believer. Conversely, Paul's gospel did not call for a Matthean concern for a body of Jesus-traditions because Paul's believer was not a disciple of Jesus but a participant in the event. To contrast Matthew and Paul is not to declare one to be "better" than the other, but it is to see that they differ and that each has his own internal coherence.

Paul thinks holistically, in terms of the structures or wholes: Adam and Christ, Israel and gentiles, law and grace, Spirit and flesh, etc. Each of these polarities is a structure of existence in which one participates, in which one's existence is defined because the participant is, by definition, "open" to and governed by the structure. The fact that these structures stand over against one another accounts for the either/or quality of much of Paul's thinking. Paul never understands the self to be autonomous, having the option of whether or not to participate in a structure. Paul's gospel therefore announces that emancipation from one structure is possible because participation in another is available.

The destructive contradiction which Paul points out, therefore, is not the Matthean one between confession and deed, but between conflicting participations. This is why Romans 6 points out that the person who has been baptized into Christ's death must regard himself/herself "dead to sin and alive to God in Christ Jesus" (v. 11); this being the case, one cannot live "in sin" and "in Christ" at the same time (v. 2). Of course Paul knew that Christians still commit sins, even if they are "freed from sin" (v. 7). But Paul is not talking about a sinless, perfect existence, as his exhortation shows: "Let not sin therefore reign" (v. 12). Rather he is talking about a transfer from one domain to another. Consequently the destructive contradiction consists of failure to claim the transfer.

This thinking in terms of wholes, of structures of power in which one participates, can be seen also in the way Paul insists that whoever wants to be justified by the law has "fallen away from grace" (Gal. 5:4), for law and grace are modes of relationship which, because of the way each links one to God, are spheres of power in which one participates. As we shall see in chapter 7, this same participation-in-structures way of thinking also underlies Paul's statement in Rom. 8:7, "You are not in the flesh, you are in the Spirit." Everything depends on the kind of reality in which one participates.

One cannot simply decide not to participate in Adam, flesh, law, or sin because apart from a liberating event which incorporates the self into a new structure, such a decision would be a futile gesture. For Paul, however, the event of Jesus Christ is precisely such an alternative structure. To believe that, to be baptized into it, and to celebrate at the Table one's pariception in it—these motifs are at the heart of Paul's gospel.

Anticipation is not an alternative to participation, but its eschatological horizon. This is because for Paul the Christ-event in which one participates is the eschatological event. Here lies the difference between Paul's participation theology and that of the mystery cults; in them, the participation is in an ever-repeated cycle and so is essentially timeless. Paul understood Christ this way not because he knew Jesus had proclaimed the imminent coming of the kingdom, nor because he knew Jesus had understood that kingdom to be irrupting into human life through his mission, including exorcisms (Mark 3:20–27). Even if Paul knew these traditions he would have regarded Jesus as the eschatological event because of the resurrection.

We must bear in mind that Paul believed in resurrection as an eschatological event long before he became a Christian, for this was a basic tenet of Pharisaism, and of other types of Judaism influenced by apocalyptic. Although there was no standard scenario for the eschaton, resurrection was part of a sequence which included judgment, rejuvenation of the world, etc. To believe that resurrection had occurred in the case of Jesus meant, therefore, that the End was beginning and that the new creation was at hand. The rest of the eschatological drama would surely follow without delay. Christ is thus the beginning of the new age and those "in Christ" were participants in new creation.

Like other Christians of the time, Paul understood himself to be living between the "already" and the "not yet," somewhat the way participants in a new administration live between election day and inauguration day. Already those who participate in Christ live out of the impending future into the present. The future is no longer an extension of the present, but an alternative to it. To live by participation in what is not yet fully here is to live by anticipatory participation; it is to claim the life of the future ahead of time and so get out of step with the present. Participation accents the present accessibility of the future; anticipation accents the futurity of that in which one participates. Participation emphasizes the already, anticipation the not yet.

Paul's thinking is characterized by this dialectic between participation and anticipation. It marks not only his understanding of the sacraments, but also his ethics. Bultmann has shown that Paul's ethic is a dialectic of the indicative and the imperative—that is, the indicative states what one now is in Christ, and the imperative summons the believer to actualize what one is. Furnish (*Theology and Ethics in Paul,* p. 225) has insisted, properly, that the imperative "is not just the result of the indicative but fully integral to it." In other words, Paul's imperative is not grounded simply in what *is* ("Become what you are!") but in what *is underway*; the only way one can participate in an event still in motion is by acting with it.

PART III

WHAT PAUL FOUGHT FOR

Paul's theology was polemical because it was wrought in controversy. His letters struggle for the authentic meaning of the gospel. They never argue with persons or positions outside the Christian community, but with Christians within it. Non-Christians were addressed in Paul's preaching and in accompanying discussions (Acts 19:8–10). The more seriously the authentic meaning of the gospel was threatened, the more intense was Paul's response. Sometimes he wrote warmly (as in 1 Thessalonians 1–3); at times magnanimously (as in Phil. 1:12–18); sometimes he was sarcastic (as in 1 Cor. 4:8) or crude (as in Gal. 5:12). Paul's letters manifest his total engagement with the subject-matter, his passionate commitment to the truth of the gospel.

The controversies provoked him to rethink fundamental themes and to clarify particular aspects of the gospel which he had preached and taught. The following chapters concentrate on three theological positions for which Paul fought. We shall first see how Paul contended for faith/trust as the wholly adequate way of salvation and mode of life, then how Paul inferred a radical Christian existence from the gift of the Spirit, and finally, how his view of God's righteousness uncovered dimensions of the human dilemma. These themes are not an outline of Paul's theology. The concern is not to tabulate and organize things Paul believed but to understand the major theological issues for which he contended.

CHAPTER SIX

DIMENSIONS OF TRUST

Repeatedly Paul had to defend and interpret his understanding of faith/trust. Four major occasions elicited an especially concentrated effort. The first was at the Council of Jerusalem (Acts 15; Gal. 2:1–10); unfortunately for us, Paul's letters do not record how he made his case. The second was Paul's confrontation with Peter at Antioch (Gal. 2:11–14). The third place was Ephesus where Paul learned that Christians in Galatia were being persuaded to accept circumcision (see chapter 5) and that a similar danger existed at Philippi, to which the letter fragment in Phil. 3:2–21 responds. The fourth occasion was writing the letter to Rome, although the exact purpose of writing precisely such a letter and sending it to Rome remains disputed.

Paul's theological understanding was not worked out in a vacuum but wrought in intense struggle with alternative views which also claimed to be Christian, indeed, more Christian than his. Stendahl is right when he insists that "Paul's doctrine of justification by faith has its theological context in his reflection on the relation of Jews and Gentiles, not within the problem of how *man* is to be saved. . . . The doctrine of justification originates in Paul's mind from his grappling with how to defend the place of the Gentiles. . . ." (*Paul Among Jews and Gentiles*, pp. 26,27, his italics). This does not mean, however, that Paul's understanding of faith was not central, as Stendahl goes on to say. Rather, for precisely the reason Stendahl gave—Paul's call—his understanding of faith was the central issue because what legitimates Paul's vocation is precisely what is at the center.

Our discussion will be guided by three questions: First, is trust/faith really adequate, or must it be supplemented? Second, if salvation by trust/faith means freedom from the law, from obligation, is Paul consistent in making moral demands on his readers? That is, does the emphasis on sheer trust dissolve the necessity of doing, or conversely, does the continuing need to do (and not do) certain things compromise the competence of trust to rectify our relation to God? Third, does Paul's emphasis on faith alone not lead to "conservative ethics"?

THE ADEQUACY OF TRUST/FAITH

The earliest literary defense of the adequacy of trust/faith was also the most vigorous, namely, in the Letter to the Galatians. In Gal. 2:21 Paul concludes his comments on his previous confrontation with Peter by saying, "if righteousness [right relation to God] comes by law, then Christ died for nothing" (NEB), a reformulation of 2:16. Why does not law—living according to law—produce a right relation to God? Paul gives various answers to this question, depending on the immediate context and occasion. Because the Galatians were persuaded ("bewitched" is Paul's word, 3:1) to make their life perfect by means of circumcision (see p. 74), Paul first argued that this contradicts their own experience of the Spirit (3:1-5).

That the Galatians had entrusted themselves to God as presented in the gospel, had been baptized and so received the Spirit (see chapter 4), was not in question. In question was whether that was good enough, whether circumcision could enhance what they already received. It is difficult for us to understand why anyone could have thought so, for today non-Jews commonly have their newborn males circumcised, and the rationale for doing so has nothing to do with religion. In antiquity, however, one explanation which Hellenized Jews gave for the operation was that cutting off a bit of skin manifested disdain for the fleshly self and signaled commitment to controlling the power of the flesh. The call to circumcision was credible to the Galatians on some such basis—that this operation ratified and enhanced their commitment to the Spirit and its struggle against flesh (understood as the "lower nature," not as Paul understood it; see chapter 7). So Paul asks, How did you get the Spirit in the first place? By obeying commandments or by believing the gospel? If the latter, then the Spirit has nothing to do with "the works of the law." Law and Spirit represent different structures of reality (see chapter 5), and are mutually exclusive.

The complex exegetical argument which begins at Gal. 3:6 (part of which was discussed in chapter 5) intends to demonstrate that God's whole purpose in Christ was (a) to bring uncircumcised gentiles into right relation to God on the basis of trust/faith and thereby make them Abraham's children; (b) to show that the promised Spirit is received on the basis of faith (3:6–14). Paul then reflects on the relation between the law and God's promise to Abraham, and on the meaning of being baptized into Christ (Gal. 3:15–29). In Gal. 4:1–11 Paul uses the analogy of the heir who is released from the control of trustees on the day set by the father (see p. 75). Interestingly, in this passage Paul tacitly connects being under the law of Moses with being under the law of "the elemental spirits of the universe" (the *stoicheia,* see p. 76). Apparently the Galatians not only accepted circumcision but returned to observing calendrical rites, thereby submitting to the influence of the *stoicheia* who controlled things through the heavenly spheres. It is not known whether the Galatians associated circumcision with the *stoicheia.* In any case, for Paul it all amounts to the same thing: a relapse into the domain of law.

Paul's understanding of law is complex, and we will note various aspects of it again in the last chapter. Here it suffices to see that law, *nomos,* means a way of life, a way of relating to God by meeting obligations. Although in the first instance "law" refers to the Scripture, particularly the Pentateuch, Paul's reference to the *stoicheia* shows that *nomos* is not restricted to the law of Moses. What interests Paul is the "lawness of law," whatever the particular law or obligation might be. Paul thinks phenomenologically about law. This is why he shows no concern to salvage law by distinguishing one law from another, the cultic from the moral law (e.g., the Decalogue). If one lives by law, by meeting requirements, it does not matter which law is being obeyed. To live by law, to meet obligations in order to relate rightly to God (to do "the works of the law"), is not to live by sheer trust in God's grace; in this case a right relation to God is not received as a gift, but as just reward.

Therefore whoever wants to be justified by the law has "fallen away from grace" (Gal. 5:4). If the right relation to God depends on meeting obligations, then the whole event of Christ was a waste of time, because *that* way of relating to God was there before.

So the Galatians misunderstood several things. (a) They thought that circumcision would enhance and perfect what they already had. In fact, however, they failed to realize that circumcision was "a package deal"; whoever accepts it obligates himself "to keep the whole law" (Gal. 5:3) because that is what circumcision really means. (b) They thought that accepting a requirement for perfection did not conflict with the mode of trust/faith. In fact, however, they failed to realize that meeting requirements and sheer trust in God do not mix. (c) They thought they could accept circumcision and revert to calendrical observances without jeopardizing the meaning of Christ. In fact, however, they failed to realize that doing so annulled the whole meaning of the Christ-event. (d) They thought that by circumcision they were dealing effectively with the power of the flesh. What they did not realize, however, is that an operation on the body cannot deal with the power of the flesh; rather, the way to deal with that is to live by the Spirit (Gal. 5:16–26)—which they already had received. (e) They thought they were fulfilling the law by being obedient to God's will in Scripture. What they did not realize, however, is that the law is fulfilled in one command—"You shall love your neighbor as yourself"— and those who have the Spirit fulfill it precisely because they are not *under* the law (Gal. 5:14,18). In short, by trying to improve sheer trust/faith, by refusing to believe that trust in God was adequate for a right salvific relation to God and to the self, the Galatians gained religiosity—but forfeited the gospel.

The important recent book by E. P. Sanders, *Paul and Palestinian Judaism,* argues "that righteousness by faith . . . serves primarily as a negative argument against keeping the law as sufficient or necessary for salvation" (p. 492), and that "the real bite of his theology lies in the participatory categories" (see chapter 5), not in the juridical ones, which deal with law and justification, though he recognizes that Paul links them (p. 502), and that ultimately they amount to the same thing (pp. 506,508). However, righteousness by faith does not have primarily a negative function. Actually, the critical function of Paul's arguments affirms the adequacy of trust/faith and is therefore simultaneously positive. As we saw (pp. 50ff.), trust constitutes the self and trust in God as interpreted in the gospel reconstitutes the self and its relation to its ground. A resolute affirmation of this insight will always appear "negative" over against every other mode of relating to God, especially those modes which slip in "doing" as a necessary supplement.

In other words, the immediate occasion of Paul's polemical argument on behalf of faith was the demand for circumcision, but that occasion was really paradigmatic. Just as Pauline trust/faith was congruent with Abraham's, so today's trust/faith is Pauline/Abrahamic when it aggressively refuses to rely on anything other than God's grace as announced in the gospel. Theologically the demand for "circumcision" can take many forms. It appears whenever one thinks along these lines: "Faith in Christ is fine as far as it goes, but your relation to God is not really right and your salvation not adequate unless. . . ." It does not matter how the sentence is completed. Whenever such fine print is introduced to qualify trust/faith, there is "circumcision" and Paul's defense of the adequacy of trust/faith is necessary.

FAITH'S FREEDOM AND THE OBLIGATION TO LOVE

Paul's polemic against the "works of the law" as a prerequisite to the right relation to God can generate the impression that, on the one hand, Paul dissolved moral obligation altogether ("You are not under law but under grace"; Rom. 6:14), and on the other hand, that he was inconsistent by also insisting that Christians live according to certain norms. Moreover, Paul can even use the phrase "the law of Christ" (Gal. 6:2; 1 Cor. 9:21). If we do not grant that Paul was fundamentally inconsistent, as I do not, then we must see how faith's freedom from the law and moral obligation cohere in Paul's thought. In other words, our theme concerns the relation of Pauline faith and Pauline ethics. We will first reflect on Paul's overall stance, then look at a specific instance.

Several aspects of Paul's stance are important. First, we have seen that for Paul there is no autonomous self, a person wholly free from sovereignty and its obverse, obligation. To be a person is to be in a sphere of influence, to have one's existence shaped by a controlling factor outside the self. Paul implies that obligation is built into humanness, for obligation is the correlate of sovereignty. Accordingly, trust/faith does not abrogate obligation categorically, nor emancipate one from obligatory norms absolutely. Rather, trust/faith in God, and the attendant life in Christ and in the Spirit, transfers the self to another domain, where Christ is the norm because he is the Lord. This transferal from one domain to another, both of which entail obligation, underlies the whole argument in Romans 6. Being emancipated from the domain of sin means being "enslaved" to God and to a new righteousness. Obligation is now defined by this new situation, and by its Lord. In other words, Paul's ethics is intimately linked with Christology and soteriology.

Second, when Paul wrote of "the law of Christ" he did not simply substitute Christ for Moses. That would be only a cosmetic change in the human situation. Sanders rightly points out that the righteousness in Christ is different because it is in Christ and so depends on trust/faith (p. 551). Phil. 3:10 clearly contrasts two kinds of rectitude: "my own, based on law" and "that which is through faith in Christ, the righteousness from God that depends on faith." Were this not the case, being baptized into Christ would be only a changing of the guard and the old way of becoming right before God would still be in effect. Under law, meeting God-given obligation was a way of attaining a right relation to God. But for whoever is rightly related to God by trust/faith, obligation is not a means to an end but the daily actualization of the end already reached by anticipation. Precisely because it is reached by trust which leans into the future for its vindication on judgment day, the right relation to God is not a manifest goodness to which one could point, but something that must be made actual constantly. Hence, Paul exhorted the Philippians, "work out your own salvation with fear and trembling; for God is at work in you" (Phil. 2:12–13). "Work out" does not mean "devise," but make effective, make actual.

The ethical meaning of the already/not yet is the dialectic of the indicative and the imperative: You are in Christ, live in Christ.

Ridderbos (*Paul,* p. 254) correctly says that the relation of the indicative to the imperative must not be reversed. One does not strive to live by the Spirit in order to be in the Spirit. Indeed, the shift from being in the domain of law to being in the domain of grace reverses the relation of the indicative to the imperative. As Paul sees it, in the domain of law where "doing" prevails, the imperative is supposed to lead to the indicative (but does not; Rom. 7:10), but in the domain of grace where trust/faith prevails, the indicative generates the imperative.

Contemporary ethicists have repeatedly argued whether an "ought" can be derived from anything other than an "is," the given, say, biological makeup. An externally derived obligation is probably unattainable—like requiring a turtle to fly. But for Paul, the "is" (the indicative) is an "is" of eschatological existence imparted by the Spirit to those who believe. Therefore the "ought" which arises from this "is" is discontinuous from obligations arising from an empirical "is," at least in certain aspects. Because there is new creation, the ethic of Christian existence appears so strange and discontinuous from the ethic of this world (see 1 Cor. 4:11–13; 2 Cor. 11:30). In other words, Paul's obligatory norm is not grounded in the potentiality of this age but in that of the age to come, in which the believer participates by trust/faith. Yet it is shaped by the tension between this age and the next (see below).

Third, because Paul is not a proto-Marcionite, the will of God for the age to come cannot be pitted against the will of God as made known in this age. Accordingly, Paul appropriates certain fundamental moral mandates accepted in the current world, and never indicts the content of the law but rather insists that it is holy, just, and good (Rom. 7:12). What was right in the law of Moses cannot be contrary to what life in Christ should produce. Rather, the Christ-event occurred "in order that the just requirement of the law might be fulfilled in us, who walk not according to the flesh but according to the Spirit" (Rom. 8:4). Elsewhere Paul identifies this core of the law as the command to love the neighbor (Rom. 13:8–10; Gal. 5:14). Since also Judaism regarded this command as the summation of the law, we must ask, "How did becoming a Christian change this point?" It changed the domain in which the love-command is heard. According to Rom. 8:4, the right obligation is fulfilled by those who have the Spirit. According to Gal. 5:22 love is the fruit of the Spirit, and according to 1 Corinthians 13 it is the chief gift of the Spirit. Paul does not mean that the Spirit simply helps the Christian do what the law requires, as if one were still in the old aeon. Were that the case, then the relation of the self to law's obligation to love would not have been changed at all; only the self's capacity would have been enhanced. But the game plan would be the same. Rather, the Spirit is the power of the new age, present in the midst of the old; it is power for moral action in the domain of the new creation, of which it is the pledge. Therefore "the just requirement of the law" is to be fulfilled by those whose life in the Spirit anticipates new creation. Unless this is clear, one understands the Spirit as a booster in one's capacity to do the will of God under the aegis of the old age in which one seeks to establish a right relation to God by achievement.

Paul's understanding of faith does not dissolve obligation, nor does his understanding of obligation undermine his contention that faith is adequate to relate one rightly to the righteous God. When the Epistle of James polemicizes against a separation of faith from works, and contends that one "is justified by works and not by faith alone" because "faith apart from works is dead" (Jas. 2:14–26), it is not Paul that is hit by this salvo but a vulgarized "Paul" who has been distorted into implying that faith is assent to doctrines. Paul's sense of moral obligation is not one iota weaker than that of James. For Paul obligation is grounded in the Christ-event and in the impingement of the new creation on the present age whose time is running out, whereas for James obligation is not grounded christologically at all. Therefore obligation in Paul is actually stronger.

We turn now to a specific instance in which Christian freedom from the domain of law manifests itself in the obligation to love within the new creation. Paul's understanding of Christian freedom must be distinguished from all views which regard freedom as absence of restraint so that the self can be fulfilled, and which see the limits of freedom where self-actualization impinges on the freedom of another. According to a popular view, one is free when one can do as one wishes, so long as one does not harm another. In Paul's understanding of freedom, however, the self is always in a sphere of power in which one has a Lord and a brother and sister; for Paul, therefore, the brother or sister does not limit freedom but provides the occasion to make it concrete.

We see this in Paul's treatment of an issue which appears at first glance to be rather remote and "picky"—dietary matters, especially those having to do with meat "offered to idols." In antiquity there was a connection between sacrifice and slaughter. Animals sacrificed in the temples were not totally burned or given to the priests; often the meat was sold to the public after part of it was used as sacrifice. It may have been rather difficult to buy meat which had not been associated with the temple. When the Corinthian Christians discovered that this situation posed some problems, they asked Paul about them in their letter to him. He responded in 1 Corinthians 8. In 1 Corinthians 10 he deals with a closely related matter, eating sacred meals in the temple precincts. The relation between these chapters is controversial (see chapter 2). In Romans 14–15 Paul also deals with matters of diet, but there the problem is not "idol meat" but vegetarianism. Here we concentrate on 1 Corinthians 8.

Modern translations put some phrases into quotation marks because it seems clear that Paul is quoting slogans being used in Corinth, perhaps even in the letter sent to Paul. What were the Corinthians saying? (a) "All of us possess knowledge"; (b) "An idol has no real existence" because "there is no God but one"—a reference to the Shema. (c) According to 1 Cor. 10:23 another slogan was "everything is permitted"—there are no limits on freedom. (This slogan appears also in 1 Cor. 6:12, which we shall discuss in the next chapter.) These slogans suggest that the Corinthians took seriously Paul's teaching of freedom from the law and of monotheism (see p. 73); there could be no danger in eating meat that had been offered to non-existent gods. But some Corinthians did not have this knowledge (1 Cor. 8:7)—apparently they had it in their minds but not in their emotions and sensibilities. They could not eat this meat in good conscience; the associations with the shrines were simply too strong.

How did he respond? (a) Paul did not argue with the slogans, nor with the theology of those who claimed freedom to eat anything they chose. He agreed with them. Here we see how far Paul had come from Pharisaism. In v. 8 he says, "food will not commend us to God. We are not worse off if we do not eat, no better off if we do." (b) Paul did not regard the scrupulous as obstacles to be overcome but as an occasion to make Christian freedom concrete. Instead of urging the scrupulous to "get with it," he urges the free to be radically free—to be free from asserting their freedom if this means ruining a person whose conscience is "weak" (1 Cor. 8:9–13). How is the "weak" Christian destroyed by the "strong" who freely eats anything, anywhere? The reasoning is not explained here, but appears in Rom. 14:23—the weak person may be induced to "go along," to eat meat without being fully persuaded that this is permissible. Then the weak person does not act out of knowledge or the freedom of living by sheer trust in God, but out of fear of being embarrassed. Then the person who eats actually does sin, because "whatever does not proceed from faith is sin." Thereby the free person's exercise of freedom occasions sin by "ruining" a fellow Christian's relation to God. Although Paul is convinced that the free person is right, he says that if his own attitude toward food causes another Christian to violate conscience, he will become a vegetarian (1 Cor. 8:13).

The scruples of fellow Christians are not an obstacle to the exercise of freedom but the opportunity for it, because not until one is free also to forgo the exercise of one's freedom for the sake of a fellow-Christian is one really free. True freedom is not a matter of everyone seeking his or her own good ("doing one's thing" unless it infringes upon another) but a matter of seeking the well-being of another. Love is more than doing good as an act of charity; it is an act for the well-being of the brother's or sister's relation to conscience and to God.

In 1 Cor. 10:1–22 the problem appears to be somewhat different, namely, whether Christians can participate in the Lord's Supper and in sacred meals at shrines as well. Here Paul forbids double participation because he believes that pagan sacrifice is actually given to demons. 1 Cor. 10:25–33, however, is concerned with private meals, and says flatly, "Eat whatever is sold in the meat market without raising any questions on the ground of conscience." Here Paul tries to move the weak toward the position of the strong. If invited to the home of a non-Christian for a meal, one is to eat whatever is served without raising questions of conscience (v. 27). But if someone else points out that the meat had been offered to idols, one is not to eat it—again in order to respect the conscience of the person who pointed this out (vv. 28–29), presumably a fellow Christian.

Paul's overall position is clear. He himself agrees with the free and the strong. Anything may be eaten. But because not all Christians are as strong as this in faith, he will *exercise* his freedom by not *insisting* on his freedom, so that the brother's and sister's relation to God may be a matter of faith—even if it is still weak faith.

A "CONSERVATIVE" ETHIC?

Paul's ethics sometimes disturbs people on several fronts. (a) Paul's ethics is pastoral throughout, oriented to and motivated by his concern to "build up" the Christian community. Paul is not concerned with the actions of non-Christians (1 Cor. 5:12). He is interested chiefly in the impression they get of the Christian group (1 Thess. 4:11–12; also 1 Cor. 14:23–25). Although he does not limit "doing good" to Christians alone (Gal. 6:10), he does not summon the church to community service, to participate in community life as responsible citizens, to be a "servant people." Still, Paul's theology and ethics open the door for Christian involvement in society, but Paul himself did not walk through it. It would have been ludicrous if he had urged small house churches to pretend that they had civic responsibility. (b) Sanders charges that Paul's theology of righteousness by faith "does not lead to ethics" (*Paul and Palestinian Judaism,* p. 492), evidently because Paul did not make the connection explicit. One may well ask, however, whether Sanders' conclusion is not premature. (c) Paul's ethics appears to be so thoroughly influenced by his expectation of the imminent parousia that it produces a "conservative" stance, for he actually urges his readers not to change their roles in society (1

Cor. 7:17–24, 29–31). It is this passage, and the issues generated by it, that concern us here.

The passage begins with Paul's rule in all his churches: "let everyone lead the life which the Lord has assigned to him, and in which God has called him" (v. 17). Then he applies this to three situations: circumcision (vv. 18–20), slavery (vv. 21–24), and marriage (vv. 25–40). In the first two instances he concludes with an imperative, "let him/her stay put" but in the third case he merely states a preference—it is better to stay unmarried (vv. 26, 40). Paul's general reasons for insisting that both the circumcised and the uncircumcised stay as they are have become clear already; the point is: neither circumcision nor uncircumcision "counts for anything."

His word to the Christian slave is of the same order, though stated differently. The slave who becomes a Christian is the Lord's freedman though one still belongs to an earthly master; likewise the free person who becomes a Christian is Christ's slave. How one is to translate v. 21 is problematic. The RSV has, "if you can gain your freedom, avail yourself of the opportunity," but the NEB's alternative rendering is probably to be preferred (and more distressing to moderns): "even if a chance of liberty should come, choose rather to make good use of your servitude." If this is the meaning, then Paul relativized slavery and freedom. Attempts to change one's status tacitly make that status more important than it is for one whose relation to God is a matter of trust/faith. What matters is not socio-economic freedom but inner freedom in Christ.

Inner freedom which is not tied to external status in society was a common theme also among Stoics. They held that because every person bears the logos, reason, or a spark of the divine, each person can be equally free inwardly, where it counts, in order to live rationally, whether one is a king or a slave. Real freedom consists in mastering that over which one has irradicable control—the decision to live rationally and wisely. No one can confer that freedom or take it away; it is an inalienable capacity (analogous to our "inalienable right"). One can, of course, forfeit it. Nothing therefore is to be taken so seriously as to restrict the self's capacity to live by reason; especially are matters of custom, institutions, bodily needs and desires, and business interests to be regarded with suspicion because they insinuate their claims on the inwardly free self and reduce it to bondage. So the Stoics urged an inner distancing from the world and a deliberate indifference to it.

What Paul says to the slave appears to echo Stoic understanding of inner freedom; likewise his counsel to unmarried Christians expressly emphasizes the importance of being free from anxieties (v. 32). He urges "those who have wives to live as though they had none, and those who mourn as though they were not mourning, and those who rejoice as though they were not rejoicing, and those who buy as though they had no goods, and those who deal with the world as though they had no dealings with it" (vv. 29b–31). What separates Paul from the Stoics here is the eschatological horizon, manifest at the beginning and at the end of this passage (vv. 29a, 31b). In other words, the Stoic inner distancing is grounded in the nature of the self, Paul's is grounded in the eschatological hour—"the form of this world is passing away." Because this world and its institutions, structures, social status, etc. have no future, Paul urges that Christians not involve themselves in it more than they must, and to make no effort to change their socioeconomic status in it. To put Paul's counsel colloquially, "Don't hustle to join (or change) a lame-duck administration."

Many readers today have difficulty with (a) Paul's assumption that because inner freedom is what matters, attempts to change one's situation makes the externals more important than they really are, and with (b) Paul's concern for distancing oneself from the world. Resistance to both points stems from the same base—the conviction that people's inward state is in fact conditioned by their external situations. On the other hand, one should not overlook the fact that a measure of inner freedom is always available even to the oppressed, the prisoner, and the poor, and when claimed manifests itself as a certain pride and dignity.

Other readers today suspect that Paul was not as faithful to his own insights as he should have been. According to 1 Cor. 12:13 all Christians were "baptized into one body—Jews or Greeks, slaves or free" and according to Gal. 3:27–28, for them "there is neither Jew nor Greek, there is neither slave nor free, there is neither male nor female." To be in Christ is to participate in new creation in which these socio-economic distinctions have lost their significance. Why, then, did Paul not insist that one should translate this eschatological reality into present social reality? Did he refuse to draw the consequences of his own theology? Or did he overreact against those who did?

It is often inferred that the Corinthians were enthusiasts because, among other things, they did translate Paul's theology into a social program among themselves. If so, then Paul opposed them because he was convinced that until the parousia one could not live only by the "already." The new creation was accessible only by faith, not by achieving changes in social relationships. Paul denied that one was already, unambiguously, manifestly saved to the extent that one could abrogate the structures of the present world. Paul's seemingly "conservative" stance may well have been his attempt to guard against the illusions of "over-realized eschatology" which was claiming too much for the "already."

Interestingly, Paul actually assumed that some change was appropriate and necessary. Both his insistence that circumcision was really irrelevant and hence merely a matter of custom, and his indifference to food laws, show that he was in fact creating a new style of community. Moreover, in his churches women exercised leadership; the whole discussion of women wearing veils while prophesying (1 Cor. 11:2–16) assumes that they speak in church as well as the men. Unfortunately this same discussion shows that in what Paul regards as a matter of "proper" conduct, he was not as free as he could have been or should have been.

Paul's successors who wrote in his name were more conservative than he was. They not only forbade women to participate in the church services (1 Tim. 2:11–12), but also appealed to lists of household duties (Haustafel) which circulated in popular moral discourse. It is in these lists of duties, not in Paul's own letters, that we find admonitions that wives must be subject to their husbands (Eph. 5:22; Col. 3:18; Titus 2:3–5), and husbands to wives. In these materials slaves are urged to be obedient but masters considerate (Eph. 6:5–8; Col. 3:22–4:1; 1 Tim. 6:1–2). Indeed, Titus 2:9–10 is concerned about the behavior of slaves toward their masters but does not say a word about the master's treatment of the slaves. Paul was far less conservative than what was written in his name.

In the last analysis, what makes Paul appear "conservative" socially is our loss of his eschatological horizon. Once the sense of the imminent end is gone, Paul comes through as a social conservative who urges that everyone stay in his or her place regardless of how long history and society continue. Appealing to 1 Corinthians 7 to say that Paul argues against all social change actually stands the apostle on his head. Paul does not sanctify the status quo as a divinely ordained order but insists on precisely the opposite—it is doomed to pass away. Neither society's inherent goodness or rightness, nor God's sanction of the way things are, causes Paul to urge Christians not to change their relation to social structures or the social structures themselves, but the conviction that God will soon change everything anyway. Actually, then, by depriving the status quo of its divine sanction, of its inherent rightness and permanence, Paul opened the way for Christians to change the world once they ceased to rely on God's impending act to do so. Paul's ethics is really not conservative at all, but lays the foundation for an ethic of social involvement. He himself built very little on this foundation. Yet here too, one might recall Paul's own word in 1 Cor. 3:10: "According to the commission of God given to me . . . I laid a foundation and another . . . is building upon it. Let each . . . take care *how* he builds upon it."

CHAPTER SEVEN

SPIRIT AND BODY

Paul's view of Spirit and body is more easily, and more commonly, misunderstood than anything else he wrote, and the consequences are serious and extensive. Paul himself sensed it. In fact, his correspondence with Corinth is dominated by the fall-out of their misunderstanding and his attempts to correct it. Romans 8 is also important, for it mentions "Spirit" more often than any chapter in the NT.

Our discussion will clarify the source of common misunderstanding, namely, Paul's contrast between Spirit and flesh; then we will note Paul's view of body-salvation. Finally, we shall see how Paul's understanding of Spirit, body, and flesh affects his ethics. But before getting into Paul's letters, three general observations are appropriate.

We begin by reflecting on what a theological discussion of the divine Spirit involves. Christology is a theological understanding of the Jesus-event. Although classical Christology includes both the pre-existence and the post-existence of Christ, the core has remained focused on Jesus, a public figure who can be investigated according to accepted canons of historiography. Pneumatology, the doctrine of the Spirit (from *pneuma,* wind or spirit), on the other hand, is a theological understanding of what is not a public but an intensely personal experience which no one sees. At most, one can see a certain behavior, such as speaking in tongues or healing, which is regarded as a manifestation of the Spirit, but neither the Spirit nor the experience of it is an observable public datum. Not even the person having the experience can observe it. Pneumatology deals with the most intimate and sometimes intense, experience of the divine. Moreover, although for purposes of discussion one can distinguish human from divine Spirit, one cannot actually isolate one from the other in order to be sure that one is talking about only one and not the other. Consequently, the more one emphasizes the working of the divine Spirit, the more one emphasizes also one's collaboration with it. Paul appears to be the first Christian theologian who recognized this.

Second, it is difficult to appreciate the role of the Spirit in early Christianity because our own attitudes intrude. Those who, for whatever reason, are gun-shy of the Holy Spirit, charismatics, or "spiritual healing," may have difficulty appreciating the early Christian experience. The "charismatics" and their sympathizers may find that the early Christian experience differed considerably from what they prize. For example, one can as easily imagine Paul announcing a Spirit-healing service as one can imagine him throwing a Hallowe'en party.

Numerous aspects of the early Christian experience of the Spirit have been noted already and need not be repeated. Only three things should be mentioned here. (a) In the NT no one receives the gift of the Spirit privately. (b) The divine Spirit was power, a divine power divinely given, not simply heightened human power. This is why it was called the *Holy* Spirit. (c) This gift of divine empowerment was understood as a hallmark of the new age, and therefore given to every believer by definition. At the same time, some persons apparently had received an extra measure of the Spirit—the prophets, such as Agabus (Acts 11:27–28) and Philip's four unmarried daughters (Acts 21:9).

Third, Paul too can be regarded as a prophet or as a charismatic figure, although he never designated himself this way. In any case, he had visions and ecstatic experiences (1 Cor. 9:1; 14:18; 2 Cor. 12:1–4), worked miracles in the Spirit (2 Cor. 12:12) and even disciplined a wayward Corinthian *in absentia* (1 Cor. 5:3–4). What Paul fought for was not the legitimacy of the experience of the Spirit but the proper understanding of it.

SPIRIT AND FLESH

It was in Corinth that the issues became most acute. The Corinthians were drifting toward what would later become full-blown,

aggressive Christianized Gnosticism. They appear to have interpreted the Spirit in a gnosticizing way—i.e., in terms of traditional
Greek metaphysical dualism which Gnosticism intensified. The
gnostic believed that he or she *is* a spark of the divine Spirit to
begin with, and that this divine essence has been trapped in a
physical, mortal body. The body caused the divine self to forget
its nature and so forfeit its destiny. The later gnostic myths will
explain how this entrapment occurred. There is no evidence that
such myths were circulating in the Corinthian church in Paul's
day, nor that the Corinthians were using the slogan *sōma-sēma*—
the body *(sōma)* is a *(sēma)* tomb. But their thinking apparently
was moving in that direction.

Accordingly, salvation was construed as release from matter,
body, history. Nothing interested a gnostic more than one's "soul's
salvation." (Frequently, gnostics blurred the distinction between
the soul and the spirit.) If the spirit or soul were not redeemed it
would be entombed in one body after another. Salvation comes to
this entrapped self when it learns who it really is, where it came
from, what its real plight now is, and what its destiny will be when
the present body dies—the self will soar homeward to be reunited
with its divine counterpart.

Apparently, the Corinthians understood the experience of the
Spirit as a confirmation of this self-understanding. One should bear
in mind that "ecstasy" means standing outside oneself, and that
"enthusiasm" means having God within. These are simply alternate ways of verbalizing the same event: the divine enters the self,
or one's spirit leaves the body to make contact with the divine.
That is, as divine spirits the Corinthians either escaped the body
during moments of ecstasy or were contacted by invading divine
power in times of heightened enthusiasm. Speaking unintelligible
language (the "language of angels") was a sign that one's spirit
had momentarily escaped the stifling influence of the mortal body.
Those who manifested these experiences were deemed to be the
most "spiritual." The wandering preachers who undermined Paul's
influence after he departed (see p. 129) apparently traded on this
mentality.

Since Paul shared some of the same views and experiences, his problem was how to clarify and correct the misunderstandings in Corinth without denying or denigrating the experience of the Spirit itself. 1 Corinthians 2–3 shows how far Paul can go in affirming a "charismatic" understanding of Christian teaching and experience. But Paul immediately turns the affirmation into an indictment of the readers: "I could not address you as spiritual persons [*pneumatikoi,* pneumatics] but as fleshly persons" [*sarkikoi,* from *sarx,* flesh]. Paul did not accuse them of being "fleshly" because he denied that they had experienced the Spirit, but because they misconstrued its meaning. The factions which had emerged (1 Cor. 1:11–12; 3:3–4) showed Paul that they were "fleshly" because cliques emerge when people champion one leader over another because one is more impressive than the other. Doing this means relying on criteria which any observer would use. But to assess the gifts of the divine Spirit by the criteria of human culture is a self-contradiction. Such spirituality is most fleshly precisely in trying to be spiritual in the wrong way. This passage shows that Paul uses "Spirit" and "flesh" in ways that might surprise today's readers no less than his original ones.

What does "Spirit" mean in Paul's thought? To begin with, Paul shares the early Christian understanding of Spirit as eschatological gift of power; the divine presence is a gift received, not an essence released (Rom. 8:15; 1 Cor. 2:12; Gal. 3:2).

Also, he regarded the Spirit as a sign that the new age is already dawning, and receiving it is a mark of one's participation in the future. The two metaphors which express this understanding appear to be uniquely Paul's: down-payment (*arrabōn;* 2 Cor. 1:22; 5:5) and first-fruits (*aparchē;* Rom. 8:23). The *arrabōn* is not so much a guarantee (as the RSV renders it) as a pledge (as the NEB has); the word used to be rendered "earnest" as in "earnest money" in real estate. Earnest money is paid to indicate that the buyer will complete the transaction without delay. The *aparchē* language comes from the OT law which required the first of the harvest to be given to God as a token of the whole crop which is about to be ripe. In Paul's mouth, both metaphors express the conviction that the Spirit means inauguration, not consummation; both celebrate the present gift as something that points ahead, as a reality that characterizes Christian life between the "already" and the "not yet."

Because Paul never defends these metaphors, it is clear that the Corinthians did not dispute this understanding of the Spirit. They too affirmed it, because also they regarded the experience of the Spirit as anticipation of salvation. But for them, this salvation was release from the body. In other words, what divided Paul and the Corinthians was not the idea that the Spirit is a pledge of the future but the sort of future that it pledged.

Käsemann has emphasized repeatedly that Paul did not separate the gift from the Giver. That is, God remains sovereign, indeed, exercises his sovereignty in giving this gift, and does not become a dispenser of power which operates independently. Thus Spirit is field of force, a power-structure in which the recipient operates as a subject in a kingdom. Rom. 8:9 makes it clear that being "in the Spirit" as a domain of power and having the Spirit "dwell in you" are simply alternate expressions.

The letter which the Corinthians sent to Paul asked about spiritual gifts; Paul responded in 1 Corinthians 12–14. Although the word which introduces the response in 12:1, *pneumatikoi,* can be either masculine or neuter, the context indicates the latter is meant —"spiritual things." The most difficult part of these chapters is 1 Cor. 12:1–3, where Paul insists that "no one speaking by the Spirit of God ever says, 'Jesus be cursed!'" Did the Corinthians actually curse Jesus when they were under the influence of the Spirit in their assemblies? Schmithals affirmed that they did—they cursed the born, earthly Jesus because they were committed to the heavenly, spiritual Christ (*Gnosticism in Corinth,* pp. 124–30). This interpretation has found little assent; the passage remains obscure.

The rest of the discussion deals with the gifts of the Spirit, *charismata* (from *charis,* grace; the gifts are "begracements"). Paul insists that the diversity of gifts is for the common good of the community. There should be neither boasting nor sense of inferiority. So Paul compares the community with a body (see p. 61). Christians with less impressive gifts should no more feel left out than a foot should feel inferior because it is not a hand. Conversely, Christians with more impressive gifts who disdain the others are as foolish as the eye who says to the hand, "I have no need of you." Just as many diverse organs make up a body, so the church has diverse persons with diverse gifts (1 Cor. 12:4–31); the Spirit actually enhances individuality.

In this context, Paul shares the "ode to love" as the chief gift of the Spirit which all can have (1 Corinthians 13). Whereas the prized gifts of prophecy, tongue speaking, and knowledge *(gnosis)* are transient, love endures, along with faith and hope.

1 Corinthians 14 gets to the most problematic and divisive gift in Corinth—speaking in tongues and prophesying. Tongue speaking (glossolalia) is unintelligible speech, prophecy is intelligible. Paul does not want to stifle either one, but to put them in proper perspective. He prefers prophecy to tongue speaking because intelligible speech benefits the whole congregation, whereas glossolalia benefits only the individual—unless someone "translates" the sounds into something that makes sense (1 Cor. 14:1–5). Consequently, if there is no interpreter present, the tongue speaker should keep silent and speak only with himself and God (1 Cor. 14:28). Paul's counsel not only subordinates the most striking gift of the Spirit to the needs of the community, but also implies that the tongue speaker *can* hold his or her tongue (at least control the volume), that one is not simply "carried away" and has no responsibility for what happens. The same is true of prophets. V. 32 denies that the power of the Spirit puts one into a mantic state in which all self-control is lost: "The spirits of the prophets are subject to the prophets." (Interestingly, according to Gal. 5:22 self-control is one of the gifts of the Spirit!)

Paul is also concerned lest the ardor for the gifts of the Spirit **destroy the order of the church's assemblies.** If everyone tongue-speaks at once (as they apparently did), a guest will conclude that this group has gone mad (1 Cor. 14:20–23). On the other hand, because prophecy is intelligible, orderly prophesying might induce a guest to conclude that "God is really among you" (v. 25). Paul's overriding concern is that "all things be done for edification" (v. 27)—not pious sentiment ("edifying thoughts"), but for the development of the community. Paul also urges that the congregation evaluate what the prophets say and not accept everything just because a person speaks under the influence of the Spirit (1 Cor. 14:29).

Near the end of his discussion, Paul makes a little "dig" at the Corinthian enthusiasts: anyone who thinks he is a prophet or a Spirit-person should recognize that what Paul says is the Lord's command—because Paul too is a person in the Spirit. One Spirit-insight should acknowledge another. Whoever disagrees with Paul, therefore, is not as "spiritual" as he or she claims to be. One suspects that here Paul's sense of apostolic office overrides everything else; otherwise Paul too would have to accede to what the Corinthians might say in the Spirit.

Throughout his letters, Paul says almost nothing about the nature of the Spirit, its relation to God or Christ (2 Cor. 3:17 is an exception). The benediction in 2 Cor. 13:14 simply juxtaposes Father, Son, and Spirit. Strictly speaking, then, Paul's letters do not teach a pneumatology. Paul's concern is rather the theological and ethical meaning of having received the Spirit.

Having seen how Paul interprets the experience of the Spirit, we now turn to its opposite—flesh (*sarx*). For Paul, *sarx* is not identical with *sōma,* body, nor is it the substance of the body. Rather, like Spirit, flesh is a domain of power, a sphere of influence in which one lives. Failure to see this is the core of the misunderstanding mentioned at the beginning of this chapter.

Here Greek thinking can easily mislead us. Greek thought was not uniform by any means. Nonetheless, one strand of it was interested in the essence of things, something almost wholly absent from Hebraic thinking. Consequently, Greek thought concerned itself with the nature of the soul (or spirit) and its relation to mind and body. The metaphysical dualism which the gnostics emphasized was ancient already in Plato's time (5th century B.C.), but received its decisive shape in his hands. In this tradition, the body retards the capacity of the soul or spirit because their essences are incompatible. The lingering effect of Greek thought manifests itself in the unfortunate translation of Romans 8, where NEB translates "flesh" as "lower nature." This is precisely what Paul does *not* mean. Wherever flesh is understood this way, one misconstrues Paul's dualism of flesh and Spirit as a struggle between the divine Spirit and our bodies, the locus of "our lower nature."

Paul's understanding of flesh is rooted in the OT, where flesh is not a constituent element of the self, a "lower nature" at odds with a "higher nature," but a way of characterizing the whole self vis-à-vis the divine. Thus when Isa. 40:5 promises that "all flesh" will see the revealed glory of God, it refers to all humanity; when Isa. 40:6 says, "All flesh is grass" which withers in comparison with the word of the Lord, it is the transient nature of human life as such that is in view, not "lower natures." Likewise, Isa. 31:3 says, "The Egyptians are men and not God; their horses are flesh and not spirit" because "flesh" means creatureliness, transitoriness. A human, like a horse, is flesh because neither is divine. "Flesh" is not a neutral term used to describe dispassionately a "nature" or an "essence"; it is an evaluative term which signals the weakness, transitoriness, unreliability of phenomenal existence.

Second, Paul also uses "flesh" when we expect him to use *sōma,* body. For instance, "weakness of the flesh" in Gal. 4:13 means susceptibility to illness; 2 Cor. 12:7 speaks of Paul's "thorn in the flesh" (nobody knows exactly what this was); 1 Cor. 7:38 mentions "afflictions in the flesh" (RSV: "worldly troubles"), and in Phil. 1:23 "remain in the flesh" means "stay alive." Rom. 2:28 contrasts true circumcision with that which is "manifest in the flesh" (RSV: "external and physical"). Likewise, Gal. 2:20 refers to "the life I now live in the flesh." Yet even when Paul uses *sarx* this way, the term has a connotation which is devaluative, not simply neutral. There is a pathos to his use of "flesh" because it hints at primarily the creaturely, contingent, vulnerable, transient character of life. This is also clear in passages where Paul speaks of "flesh and blood" (Gal. 1:16; 1 Cor. 15:30). In all these passages, "flesh" interprets the empirical in light of the transcendent. Just as "this age" is always a valuing term in light of "the age to come," so "flesh" characterizes the empirical in light of Spirit.

In other words, the third thing to see is that Paul did not so much interpret the Spirit in light of flesh but the reverse; his understanding of the Spirit illumined what flesh really is. It is highly unlikely that Paul's understanding of flesh was part of his pre-

Christian theology, even if the OT is its formal origin. Rather, like everything else in Paul, the starting-point was Christ and the Christian experience of God's grace. E.P. Sanders is right on target when he insists that "Paul's thought did not run from plight to solution, but rather from solution to plight" (*Paul and Palestinian Judaism,* p. 443). This is as true of "flesh" as it is of "law."

Paul's understanding of flesh appears in some of his characteristic expressions. (a) A major phrase is "according to the flesh." In Rom. 8:4, walking (= living) according to the flesh is contrasted with walking according to the Spirit (so also v. 5). The contrast is implied even when only "according to the flesh" is mentioned, as in 2 Cor. 1:17 (where RSV and NEB have "like a worldly man") and 2 Cor. 5:16 (RSV: "from a human point of view"; NEB: "worldly standards"). To live "according to the flesh" is to have the norms and values of life determined by the merely phenomenal, the frail and transient instead of by the Spirit which is transcendent. (b) The same is true of the adjective "fleshly" (*sarkikos* or *sarkinos*), as in 1 Cor. 3:3 (see above). (c) Rom. 8:6 contrasts the "mind set" of the flesh with that of the Spirit. (d) "In the flesh" is the counterpart to being "in the Spirit" as Rom. 8:9 clearly says: "You are not in the flesh, you are in the Spirit." It is the Spirit as a sphere of power which has suggested that its opposite, flesh, is also a sphere of power.

Fourth, even though Paul can pit flesh and Spirit against each other (as in Gal. 5:17 or Rom. 8:7–8), he does not equate flesh and sin. The only passage which might suggest that he did is Rom. 8:3, for here he interprets the incarnation as follows: "God . . . sending his own Son in the likeness of sinful flesh . . . condemned sin in the flesh" (RSV). The phrase "sinful flesh" renders "of flesh of sin" and appears to characterize flesh itself as sinful. Yet "condemned sin in the flesh" distinguishes flesh from sin, so that it appears that the two are linked closely but not actually equated. This is why sin was condemned in its stronghold. (One should not over-interpret "in the likeness of" here, as if Paul implied that Christ assumed flesh that only looked like ours but was really different because his flesh was sinless; this introduces precisely the equation of sin and flesh which is not characteristic of Paul.) Flesh is a domain of power in which sin operates. That is why sin is condemned there. The center of the human predicament is not flesh but sin, living according to, setting the mind on, flesh.

In short, because Spirit is the power-sphere of the new age, flesh is the power-sphere of the old age. The struggle between Spirit and flesh is not a battle between higher and lower nature, between our bodily drives and our minds or spirits. Rather, the struggle is between the power of the eschatological future and the power of the empirical present.

In this light, we can now turn to Paul's understanding of body, *sōma*. For Paul, the central meaning of "body" is the actual self, what we might call the psychosomatic entity that I am. If "flesh" is a devaluing term, "body" is much more neutral. Paul never uses the phrase "according to the body." Frequently one can translate it "self." For instance, the RSV renders Rom. 12:1 literally as "Present your bodies as a living sacrifice" but the NEB correctly renders *sōma* here as "your very selves." This use of "body" appears in our term "somebody" and in the lines of the song, "When a body meets a body coming through the rye." Because Paul does not share the Greek view of the self as a spark of divine essence, he would not say "I have a body" but "I am body." Yet he does speak of "my body" (1 Cor. 9:27), hinting that one's actual existence is an object of one's action and will, that one can distinguish oneself from oneself, as Bultmann puts it (*Theology of the New Testament* I, pp. 195–6). Because *sōma* refers to the actual self and not merely to one's physical body, we need to see how Paul relates salvation to *sōma*.

BODY WITH A FUTURE

For Paul salvation is for the body, the actual self I am. Here Paul's difference from gnostic anthropology manifests itself, for Paul does not believe salvation is a release of the soul *from* the body but a redemption *of* the body (Rom. 8:23). The presence of the Spirit is a pledge of this, as Rom. 8:11 makes explicit: "If the Spirit of him who raised Jesus . . . dwells in you, he . . . will give life to your mortal bodies also through the Spirit which dwells in you." According to Phil. 3:20 it is Christ "who will change our lowly body to be like his glorious body," not extract an eternal soul from it.

The fullest exposition of Paul's understanding of body-salvation begins by reminding the readers that they had accepted the gospel centered in the death and resurrection of Christ (1 Cor. 15:1–11; see p. 34). But now some are saying, "There is no resurrection of the dead." Had they changed their minds? There is no reason to conclude that they denied the resurrection of Christ; in fact, Paul points out that what they deny contradicts what they have believed about Christ (vv. 13–19). It is likely that they denied resurrection categorically (not life after death); if so, then they probably interpreted Christ's resurrection as the release of his eternal soul or spirit from the body. In any case, for them "There is no resurrection of the dead" was not a word of despair but a triumphant assertion of the victory of spirit over matter. Like Paul, the Corinthians believed that what was true of Christ is true of themselves also. They also agreed fully with Paul, "Flesh and blood cannot inherit the kingdom of God" (v. 50). From these two agreements, however, they were drawing opposite conclusions.

Paul points out that Christ has been raised from the dead, not released from a mortal body, and that his resurrection is the first fruits of resurrection (v. 20), the prototype. What happened to Christ will happen to "those who belong to Christ" (v. 23). That is, Paul uses the agreed-on principle "as Christ, so we" against the Corinthian denial of resurrection.

In answering the questions, "How are the dead raised?" and "With what kind of body do they come?" Paul makes it clear that he understands resurrection to be transformation, not resuscitation. (This is true of the NT as a whole.) The heart of Paul's contention is "We shall all be changed" (vv. 51–2). To illustrate his point, he appeals to the transformation which a kernel of grain undergoes when it "dies": It is buried a brown seed but comes up a green plant—the same, yet different. To undergird his analogy, he points out that "not all flesh is alike" (a rare neutral use of "flesh"), in order to argue that there are also different bodies, earthly and heavenly ones (vv. 35–41). Although the rationale is not altogether cogent, what Paul is driving at is stated in v. 44: "if there is a physical body, there is also a spiritual body." So, the mortal body is planted in the ground, but it is raised "in glory"; it is planted "a physical body, it is raised up a spiritual body." Nowhere else does Paul mention this "spiritual body" and it is hard to know just what he had in mind. What is clear, however, is that a totally disembodied existence is repudiated.

In vv. 25–28 Paul had identified the final enemy to be overcome as death. In vv. 53–54, however, Paul subtly introduces another way of talking: "the corruptible" and "the mortal." Death the enemy is not the same as mortality, for the former is a usurping tyrant over human life, whereas the latter is a qualification built into the body ("flesh and blood cannot inherit. . . ."). By shifting to this terminology, Paul tacitly grants that the gnosticising perception of the human problem cannot be dismissed out of hand; if salvation is for the body-self then the inherent mortality must be dealt with. Defeating an external tyrant, death, does not yet deal with this inbuilt defect. But instead of following the Corinthian solution, Paul argues for an alternative: transformation of the mortal body. It "puts on" immortality—that is what "we shall all be changed" means. In other words, even if the human situation is understood in Greek terms, Paul solves it in Jewish-Christian apocalyptic terms, for the transformation will occur at the parousia. Thus he can cite Isa. 25:8 and Hos. 13:14, here understood as proclamations of eschatological triumph over death.

In 2 Cor. 5:1–5 Paul also discusses this eschatological transformation, but now contrasts the two modes of existence as an earthly tent and an eternal, heavenly house. The passage is somewhat obscure, but the core of the matter is clear: although Christians "groan and long to put on our heavenly dwelling," they do not desire to be "unclothed"—deprived of body categorically. Rather, the longing is to be "further clothed" so that what is mortal may become immortal. Here too the Spirit is the pledge of this transformation.

Paul shows no interest in describing the resurrection body, nor does he hint at where the new mode of existence will be lived. In 1 Thess. 4:13–17 he simply says, "the dead in Christ will rise first; then we who are alive . . . shall be caught up together with them in the clouds to meet the Lord in the air; and so we shall always be with the Lord." What interests Paul is the "thatness" of resurrection as transformation of actual human existence. In Phil. 1:21-23 he appears not even to have room for resurrection, for he speaks of being with the Lord immediately after death. How all this hangs together is not clear. He might not have been as logically consistent as we would like him to have been; it may also be that he simply called attention to certain aspects of the future hope which he deemed relevant to the argument at hand, and assumed the rest. "The rest," of course, is what we very much want to know.

What is at stake theologically is the understanding of God the Creator and of the self. Views of post-mortem existence which are based on the release of an eternal essence from a temporal, mortal body imply that the body is unredeemable, and hence they tacitly indict the Creator for making such a thing in the first place. They also imply that the divine essence is eternal, that it too pre-exists but somehow comes into a body; in other words, such views easily lead to the idea of the transmigration of eternal souls from one body to another. Difficult as Paul's view may be, it at least avoids these consequences.

BODY ETHICS

The ethical significance of Paul's theology of body manifests itself throughout his letters, but we shall consider only a few passages from 1 Corinthians and Romans. 1 Cor. 6:12-20 contains the basic theological position: "the body is not meant for immorality, but for the Lord, and the Lord for the body." Paul provides several warrants for this. First, "God raised the Lord and will also raise us up by his power. Do you not know that your bodies are members of Christ?" Paul's rationale seems to be the following: (a) Christ's resurrection transformed him (as *sōma/ self*). (b) His resurrection is the prototype of resurrection to come, of Christian somatic selves. (c) Christ's present Lordship lays a claim on the body/self, destined for resurrection. Second, because body = self, Paul can express this claim by saying that the *sōma* of the Christian is an organ ("member") in the body of Christ. Third, "your body is a temple of the Holy Spirit within you." The mortal body/self is not a prison for the Spirit but its shrine. The body/ self does not inhibit the Spirit; the Spirit, being stronger, sanctifies the body/self. Sanctification is not an intense religious experience but a moral process which hallows the self. Fourth, "you are not your own; you were bought with a price"—a metaphor derived from the slave market. Redemption means belonging to Christ, whose death was the (implied) price paid. So the moral meaning of having the Spirit is the imperative: "glorify God in your body" —the actual selves you are. Paul's ethics is body-ethics.

All this was said over against the Corinthian trend, which spawned two opposing ethics. On the one hand, if one believed that the gospel brought to light one's essence as Spirit, and if one regarded baptism in a hyper-sacramental way (see p. 58), then one could develop a free-wheeling ethic. One could proclaim "I am free to do anything." If the Lordship of Christ has to do with the eternal Spirit in the self, then it does not matter what one does with one's body. Indeed, one might even make it a point of demonstrating freedom by deliberately violating customs, taboos and laws which control activities of the body. On the other hand, if one believed that the physical body was inherently hostile to the Spirit, then one might develop an ascetic ethic designed to thwart the body and its drives. The Corinthians pursued both strategies; inevitably, matters of sex and marriage brought the issues to a head.

The former style probably explains the case of the man who married his stepmother, contrary to both Jewish and Roman law (1 Cor. 5:1–2). Evidently she was not a Christian, for Paul says nothing to *her* (in accord with 1 Cor. 5:12). Beyond excluding *him* from the group, it is not clear exactly what disciplinary action Paul called for (vv. 3–5). More important, some Corinthians evidently were proud of him for he dared to live out his theology. His action is not the consequence of Corinth being "that kind of place," but a deliberate strategy designed to manifest his self-understanding.

The latter style led other Corinthians to write Paul about sex and marriage. Paul's response is in 1 Corinthians 7, parts of which have already been discussed (see p. 98). It is not clear whether the opening statement in v. 1 is a slogan in Corinth (as the alternate translation in the NEB has it, as well as the Jerusalem Bible) or whether it is Paul's own view: "It is well for a man not to touch a woman." Either way, he agrees with it as a general principle—but then he ignores it as he deals with the problems at hand. Instead of explicating the metaphysical or moral rationale of this principle and then applying the result to the questions asked, Paul proceeds in an eminently practical, down-to-earth manner. In other words, Paul affirms sexual continence as a "good" but regards it as a special gift of the spirit (one of the *charismata*), not something that applies to everyone (1 Cor. 7:7-8).

Paul's views of sex and marriage, when gauged by modern sensibilities, are often disdained. Yet in his context, they are much less male-dominated than similar treatments by Cynic-Stoic contemporaries or parts of the Jewish Wisdom tradition.

The Jerusalem Bible brings out the point of 1 Cor. 7:2: "since sex is always a danger. . . ." Nowhere in the entire discussion is there any positive assessment of sex as a means of enhancing mutuality or of expressing love and tenderness. But such a view of sexuality is a modern one, and we must no more expect to find it in Paul than we should expect him to advocate dental hygiene. In light of the Corinthian options, his views are rather "advanced." Paul does recognize that sex is a powerful drive, and he refuses to concede that having the Spirit neutralizes its power. So he tells the Corinthians that, given the dynamics of sex, everyone should be married (v. 2), unless one has the special Spirit-gift capacity to remain single. That singleness may be chosen for other reasons perhaps never crossed his mind.

Paul then discusses sex within marriage (vv. 3-6). The point is that husband and wife belong to one another; neither is to regard the other as an object for self-gratification. Neither is to deny the other the "right" to sex. Moreover, if one of them should insist on refraining from sexual activity for the sake of religious devotion (like giving it up for Lent), this must be by mutual consent, and for a limited time only. Not only does Paul insist on parity within marriage in a way that was considerably ahead of his time, but he tacitly says, "Don't think you are so 'spiritual' that you can forgo (or be denied) sex indefinitely without serious consequences. You are not *that* saved." In other words, Paul's advice to couples is designed to disabuse them of their illusions about sex and the Spirit. He refuses to allow religious devotion to become the pretext for withholding sex from one's spouse.

In vv. 8–9 Paul counsels the unmarried and widows to remain single, but if their sexual drives create frustrations, they should marry "for it is better to marry than to burn" (with frustrated passions). This strikes moderns as a rather low, utilitarian view of marriage; the current mode of dealing with the situation—cohabitation without marriage—is not even discussed, for it never entered Paul's mind as a viable option. Paul's view of marriage is not a romantic one, to be sure, but again it must be seen for its impact in Corinth. Paul offers not a word of solace to those who, in the name of the Spirit, take it upon themselves to deny fulfillment of sexual drives. Precisely the opposite. He urges people to avoid frustration, not by hyper-spirituality, but by getting married! The highly problematic passage in vv. 36–38 makes the same point with reference, apparently, to the engaged: "Let them marry—it is no sin."

The parity which Paul advocated for the Christian man and wife he extended also to households where only one of them is Christian (vv. 12–16). If either non-Christian spouse is willing to stay married, the Christian should not seek divorce. Clearly Paul does not want the gospel to break up households; his attitude is quite different from that of Matt. 10:34–37. Moreover, Paul believes that the sanctity of the Christian spouse is imparted to the non-Christian spouse; otherwise, "your children would be unclean, but as it is they are holy" (v. 14). Unfortunately Paul's rationale is not stated as clearly as it might have been, but the main point is manifest: the Christian is not defiled by having sex with a non-Christian spouse; one does not have to protect the Spirit. Nonetheless, if the non-Christian spouse wants a divorce, one is not to contest it. Paul makes it clear that this is his word, not the Lord's (v. 12).

He makes it equally clear that it is not he but the Lord who commands that Christians not divorce each other (v. 10), but then adds a revealing phrase, "but if she does . . ." (and implies "but if he does . . ."). Paul is aware that in the changed circumstances of Corinth, he cannot insist on literal compliance with the word of

Jesus, and that "mixed marriage" is something Jesus never had to face.

In 1 Corinthians 7 Paul's body-ethic expresses itself in his concern to give constructive counsel designed to enhance marriage and family life. Not a word appears about the evils of the body or of sexuality; not a line encourages the Corinthians' ascetics for metaphysical reasons. There is not a hint that the Spirit might be diminished by normal family life or that it makes family life impossible. In vv. 32–35 he does point out that concerns for domestic life might well distract from concern for "affairs of the Lord" just as he says that this world has but little time left (vv. 29–31; see p. 96). But these are practical considerations, not metaphysical ones. Paul's body-ethic is not negative, even though he clearly rejects certain behavior without ado (1 Cor. 5:11; 6:9–10).

Finally, Paul's body-ethic calls for a new attitude toward suffering. According to Rom. 8:18–25, having the Spirit does not immunize one against the world's suffering but actually enlivens the awareness of participating in it. Paul alludes to Genesis 3, according to which God "cursed" the ground, along with Adam and Eve: creation was "subjected to futility" and now exists in "bondage to decay." Yet because Paul thinks telically (see p. 75), he insists that God's action was not the last word, for this subjection is to be terminated, evidently at the parousia when creation will be liberated and transformed. In the meantime, creation groans, yearns for redemption. Paul says all this to set up v. 23: those who have the Spirit also groan, like creation, as they wait for the future redemption of the body/self. Because the body/self is part of creation, the more intense the experience of the Spirit, the more awareness of the yet unredeemed character of existence, all of it. Paul implies that just as Christ's resurrection is the first fruits of the redemption of body/selves, so the existence of Spirit-bearing selves is the first-fruits of the redemption of all creation. The presence of the Spirit is an assurance of God's commitment, and so Christians need have no fear of suffering for it cannot separate them from God (Rom. 8:31–39). How could it, when God's own Son suffered as part of the God-given mission to redeem creation? In this light, Paul can say that "we rejoice in our sufferings"—not because we enjoy them but because the Spirit has been given so that now suffering can yield a positive moral meaning (Rom. 5:1–5). Suffering is no longer an index of how one stands with God (Job's problem); rather, how one stands with God is an index of how one may regard suffering.

CHAPTER EIGHT

THE MORAL INTEGRITY OF GOD AND THE HUMAN SITUATION

Believing in God is not enough. Everything depends on the God in whom one believes and to whom one entrusts his or her life. Paul saw this clearly.

The Christ-event, centered in Jesus' cross and resurrection, revealed God decisively and thereby uncovered the character of the human situation as well. The cross/resurrection was the hub to which all spokes of Paul's theology were joined; procedurally, the cross/resurrection was the starting-point for Paul's theological thinking. Paul did not, and could not, fit the Christ-event into the understanding of God which he inherited. Rather, his encounter with Christ compelled him to rethink everything from the ground up (which is not to say that he repudiated his heritage). As Sanders noted (see p. 107) Paul did not work out his theology as a solution to a set of problems with which he had been wrestling unsuccessfully; rather, it was in light of the universal salvation wrought by cross/resurrection that he discerned the real character of the human problem.

Christian apologists commonly begin by first analyzing the human situation in categories which the non-Christian, it is hoped, will acknowledge; then they present the Christian faith as an answer. We do not know whether Paul used this strategy in his preaching, as Acts 17 in fact has him do (unsuccessfully!). His letters, however, show his thought moving in the opposite direction —from solution to plight. The title of this chapter reflects that movement of thought.

We shall first probe Paul's understanding of God as the rectifier of the ungodly. Then we shall see how Paul's insight into the character of God illumined the human situation. Finally, we shall note how the character of God affected Paul's attitude toward the future. Inevitably, many aspects of these themes have been touched before. It is appropriate, however, to bring some of the threads together in a discussion of the heart of Paul's theology for which he contended.

THE RECTIFIER OF THE UNGODLY

One of the most radical understandings of God in the NT cannot be found in a concordance because the term "God" is not used —namely, the one "who justifies the ungodly" (Rom. 4:5). This statement is of a piece with other characterizations of God in the same chapter: (a) the one "who gives life to the dead and calls into existence the things that do not exist" (v. 17); (b) the one who "raised from the dead Jesus our Lord" (v. 24). Like Rom. 5:8, these formulations express Paul's keen awareness that the cross and resurrection reveal the disparity between God and the prevalent understandings of God. The Christ-event disclosed the God one can really count on because it made clear God's commitments and his capacity to keep them, his moral integrity.

The adjective "moral" should not be taken to mean that God is "moral." Rather it simply distinguishes what is in view here from ontic integrity—the oneness and unity of God's being. The unity of God's being is not something Paul discussed or defended in his letters; they show no awareness that statements about Christ as the Son of God or the Wisdom of God in any way compromised monotheism. What Paul did contend for is the constancy, consistency, dependability, trustworthiness, faithfulness of God in light of Jesus' cross and resurrection. It is these aspects of the integrity of God which the term "moral" indicates in the phrase "the moral integrity of God." When is God's Godhood most characteristically and significantly manifest? When God is true to himself, what happens to the world? To reflect on such themes is to reflect on the moral integrity of God.

"The moral integrity of God" is not Paul's phrase, of course; it restates the point of a phrase which he did use—the righteousness of God. To grasp Paul's radical understanding of God therefore requires us to attend to rather technical philological matters, though only the most salient can be noted here.

We may begin with the semantic problem created by the limitations of the English language. "Righteousness" and "justice" are used to translate the same Greek word which Paul used, *dikaiosynē*; similarly, "righteous" and "just" render the same adjective *dikaios*. However, to translate the verb *dikaioō* we use the Latin "justify" since we cannot say "rightify." But righteousness and justice do not mean exactly the same things, and certainly "justify" commonly does not mean "to make right" but to provide reasons for, even excuses ("He is justifying himself again."). Given the divergence between justice and righteousness in common parlance, it is inevitable that most people make no connection between righteousness and justification. But in Paul's usage, they are simply different semantic forms of the same idea. When Kendrick Grobel translated Bultmann's *New Testament Theology,* he proposed using the old English term "rightwise" for "justify"; however, "rectify" is less archaic and will be used here. In other words, to justify is to rectify, make right—not just (fair, equitable).

Although Paul wrote Greek, his meanings are derived from the OT and its understanding of right, righteous, etc. (a) The Hebrew term *ts-d-q,* and its various forms, refers to a relationship, to a norm, not to an inherent quality which we might call "righteous" or good. Righteousness is rightness. The specific meaning of righteous/ righteousness depends on the norm in view. For example, in Genesis 38, the widow Tamar dressed like a whore in order to seduce her father-in-law Judah because according to Hebrew law he should have arranged for her to marry the deceased's brother in order to have children (for reasons of social and economic security in that society). Deprived of her "rights" she managed to become pregnant with Judah. When confronted by this situation, Judah said, "She is more righteous than I"—not meaning that she is morally better but that she was more in right relation to the norm than he had been. To be *ts-d-q* is to keep faith with what is right, with what is the right thing to do for the persons involved.

(b) In this light, we can understand Judg. 5:11 which speaks of

God's military victories over the Canaanites as his "righteous-nesses" (note the plural!)—events in which God did what was right by his people in light of his covenant commitments. Similarly, when Isa. 51:5 puts in parallel lines (indicating virtual equivalent meaning) "my *ts-d-q*" and "my salvation," it is clear that righteous-ness means God's deliverance (RSV) which accords with what is right for him to bring about. Such deliverance manifests the in-tegrity of God; his keeping commitments.

(c) A verbal form of the Hebrew means "to make right," to rectify a relationship; in judicial matters it means "declare to be in the right" (as in "on the right side of the law"). It does not mean "make righteous" in the sense of making "good." If one is falsely accused and acquitted, one is "justified"—declared to be in the right after all, vindicated, as in Isa. 43:26, where God urges, "Set forth your case, that you may be proved right" (justified). Amos had a vision of a leaning wall, doomed to fall because it was not plumb (upright). Had his vision included an alignment to the plumb line, he could have said that the wall was "justified"—made right (not made a good wall). The same usage underlies Jesus' comment about the publican in the temple who confessed his sins, "this man went down to his house justified"—his relation to God had been made right. In such cases "to justify" means to correct, to rectify a relation to a norm, to align properly. Interestingly, there is one English usage of "justify" which is very similar—the electric typewriter that "justifies" the margins—aligns all the lines of type. In short, to justify is to rectify the relation to the norm; justifica-tion is rectification.

(d) It is one thing to speak of human relationships to a norm, but what does it mean to speak of the "righteousness of God"? By what norm is God to be judged? and who is the judge of the matter? Or does "righteousness of God" mean something quite different from the righteousness of a person? The meaning of "righteousness of God," especially in Paul, has been debated vigor-ously in recent years. On the surface, the debate has been over a grammatical point—how to take "of." But the issues at stake are far-reaching.

Käsemann has challenged Bultmann's view that the phrase always denotes the righteousness which comes from God to the believer (Käsemann's essay in *New Testament Questions of Today,* pp. 168–182). Rom. 10:3, literally translated, reads "for not knowing the righteousness of God, and seeking to establish their own righteousness, they did not submit to the righteousness of God." The RSV renders it "being ignorant of the righteousness *that comes from* God" and the NEB has "they ignore God's way of righteousness." The RSV and Bultmann appear to be supported by Phil. 3:9 where Paul writes of the righteousness that comes from God to the believer, a new right relationship which is granted by God. Käsemann did not dispute this point, but insisted that Rom. 3:25–26 does speak of God's *own* righteousness. Rather than conclude that Paul used the same phrase in two senses, he sought an understanding of the phrase which underlies both. He found it in the OT and in Jewish apocalyptic, where God's righteousness means his rectifying activity vis-à-vis the world. Käsemann's reconstruction of the morphology of this meaning has been criticized; nonetheless, when the dust settles he will be more "justified" than not.

Having oriented ourselves to the major problem of Paul's "righteousness" language, we can now take up the central question, What has the righteousness of God—the moral integrity of God—got to do with the rectification of the human relation to God? Here Rom. 3:25–26 is basic (see p. 75), although difficult to translate. The RSV has Paul say that the Christ-event occurred "to show God's righteousness, because in his divine forbearance he had passed over former sins; it was to prove at the present time that he himself is righteous and that he justifies him who has faith in Jesus." Not only does this obscure the fact that "to show" and "to prove" are virtually identical phrases in Greek, but it shifts from "righteous" to "justify" (for reasons noted above). The NEB, on the other hand, gains semantic consistency but jeopardizes the meaning: "to demonstrate his justice . . . to demonstrate his justice now . . . showing that he is both himself just and justifies. . . ." A more exact rendering is: "to demonstrate his rectitude . . . to demonstrate his rectitude . . . so that he might be in the right by rectifying. . . ." The rectitude of God, his moral integrity, manifests itself in rectifying the relation between himself and persons. God's Godhood comes through in justification; God is never more authentically and characteristically God than when he "rectifies the ungodly."

What sort of God rectifies the godly, the pious, the religious? Such a God would be most faithful to himself, would manifest his moral integrity by rewarding the godly, religious folk who kept all the rules. Such a God would be the patron of a religious community, or of an ethnic or racial group. Moreover, if God rectified the godly, he would be calculable and controllable, because an achievement-reward system can be manipulated. Then rectification would be in human hands—those would be in right relation to God who made that relation right. Also, if the rectifier of the godly did not punish all the ungodly he would treat certain persons or groups as exceptions, as special cases. But then God's moral integrity would be undercut, for he would show favoritism.

What, then, does it mean to believe that God rectifies the ungodly? First, he is not committed to vindicating his clients, his group, party, nation, but to making right precisely everyone who is wrongly related to him. Because to be godly is to be like the God we image, each person or group regards God as the vindicator of its values. This makes God the opponent of those we oppose, the ultimate warrant of human power struggles, wars, acts of self-aggrandizement. God's moral integrity is therefore measured by the success of his clients. But if God is the rectifier of the ungodly, then his moral integrity is measured solely by his own character and commitments—"his ways are not our ways." If God rectifies the ungodly, then the persons who need rectification are not others, other groups, the outsiders, the enemy, but everyone whose relation to God is not right. If God rectifies the ungodly, then "God shows no partiality" (Rom. 2:11), and is not the God of the Jews only or any other group (Rom. 3:29), and his wrath is against "*all* ungodliness and wickedness" (Rom. 1:18).

Second, if God rectifies the ungodly, then God exercises his sovereignty in freedom (see p. 73). But the freedom of God is not his capacity to be arbitrary, for that would annul his moral integrity. Only a righteous God who is free to be faithful to himself and to his commitments is capable of rectifying the ungodly, because in doing that his own rectitude becomes effective. Implicit in

Paul's insight is the independence of God from all human domestication, the radical otherness of God from all human effort to make God in our image, and the freedom of God to rectify precisely the relation to a wrongly-imaged God. A God who cannot do this is really an ideological no-god, a tribal deity of class, race, sex, or power block.

Paul's understanding of the righteousness of God who rectifies the **ungodly** is grounded in Jesus' cross/resurrection, as Rom. 4:25 makes clear: Jesus "was put to death for our trespasses and raised for our justification" (rectification). The discontinuity between the God who justifies his godly clients and the God who rectifies the ungodly is grounded in the fact that God resurrected a Jesus who died under a curse. In Gal. 3:13 Paul quotes Deut. 21:23, "cursed be everyone who hangs on a tree," which he interprets as a reference to the crucifixion. Therefore Christ became "a curse for us" —that is, he died as a cursed man (on the "for us" see p. 53). Because Jesus was executed as one accursed by the law, the resurrection of precisely this Jesus reveals that God's verdict on him cannot be inferred from the cross. Were that the case, God would indeed rectify the godly who put him there in the name of the law, and in the name of law and order. But Jesus' resurrection reveals God's freedom and otherness. Moreover, unless God's resurrecting Jesus was arbitrary (unthinkable to Paul), the resurrection must reveal God's fidelity to Jesus and to himself; that is, it revealed God's integrity over against what was presumed to be his integrity. The fact that the Christ-event occurred in a sinful world shows Paul that God is free to rectify the world and persons in it, and that this rectification does not depend on human readiness, achieved goodness, or self-wrought rectitude but solely on God's grace. Whoever trusts this God is therefore not only rightly related to God (rectified), but must realign every conception of God and of the human condition according to this event.

THE FAILURE OF LAW

If *anyone* who trusts the God of the gospel is rightly related to God (rectified), then preaching-trusting overcomes the *universal* human dilemma. Otherwise, the Galatians would have been right—

trust/faith would be competent only to a certain extent or in limited areas of life, and would need to be supplemented (see p. 85f.). Moreover, the parity of all persons in trust/faith implies a solidarity in the human predicament, for the same resolution implies the same dilemma. Paul is thoroughly consistent: "there is no distinction; since all have sinned and fall short of the glory of God" (Rom. 3:22–23).

Furthermore, there is a "law of parsimony" in soteriology—the solution goes as far as, but no farther than, the dilemma. If the human plight is essentially ignorance of what one must do, then it is enough to provide knowledge of it; there is no need for an atonement. If we put alongside this consideration another, that the resolution defines the plight, then the question arises: How deeply into the human dilemma does Paul's understanding of salvation penetrate?

The core of the human dilemma for Paul is the incapacity of law to produce a right relation to God, one of trust/faith. For Paul, law fails, not because there is something inherently wrong with it (were that the case, the answer would be to get rid of the law) but because it is frustrated by another reality, sin. Because Paul regards death as the "wages of sin" (Rom. 6:23), the human situation is bounded by sin, death, and law—interrelated domains of power.

Rom. 5:12–21 became one of the most fateful passages Paul wrote, for it shaped Augustine's doctrine of original sin, in turn restated by Luther and Calvin. Actually, here Paul is less interested in accounting for sin than in showing the surpassing power of salvation. The passage is structured by comparisons of Adam and Christ, and the consequences of their deeds. Behind Paul's discussion of Adam and Christ stand not only Genesis 3 but Jewish interpretations of Adam, which in turn may have been influenced by the ancient myth of the Primal Man (see Scroggs, *The Last Adam*).

According to Rom. 5:12 "sin came into the world through one man and death through sin, and so death spread to all men because all men sinned." The RSV's "because" renders an expression which the Latin translates as *in quo,* and which Augustine took as "in whom" (all men sinned). Most recent interpreters agree with the RSV; Paul did not teach "In Adam's fall, we sinned all," but rather that ever since Adam everyone sins. Paul shows no interest in the question of how "original sin" (not his phrase) spread. What does interest him is the universality of sin and the parity of all persons with regard to it (Rom. 5:18–21).

Paul speaks of sin as if it were a person because he regards it as a tyrant with a power-sphere. Although he writes of "trespasses" in order to bring out the concreteness of disobedience, it is sin that interests him, not particular sins or wrong-doings. According to Paul, we do not sin because we are mortal, because mortality generates *Angst* (anxiety), which in turn generates specious mechanisms which are sinful; rather, we have become subject to death because of sin. Because everyone participates in sin's domain by sinning, everyone is an accomplice in death's tyranny, not an innocent victim, even though death "reigned" as a tyrant (Rom. 5:14,17,21). Because the domain of sin and the domain of death are intimately linked, Paul can say that whoever "has died is freed from sin" (Rom. 6:7). To participate in Christ's death, therefore, is to participate in his liberation from death, and hence from sin, because "death no longer has dominion over him" (Rom. 6:9). In the domain of sin and death, sins are a concrete manifestation of a state of bondage; in the domain of Christ, sins manifest an inconsistency in the status. The tension between the "already" and the "not yet" means that one must struggle to be obedient to the Lord of the new domain (Rom. 6:15–22). Therefore whoever participates in Christ's death and expects to share his resurrection-transformation must now consider himself or herself "dead to sin and alive to God in Christ Jesus" (Rom. 6:11). This "considering" is not a pretending that it is true in order to see what happens, but a claiming by faith and obedience the newness and freedom of the new age. When one struggles against sin on this basis, "sin will have no dominion over you, since you are not under law but under grace" (Rom. 6:14). Christians are not made incapable of sinning (Gal. 6:1); rather, sin no longer is the determinative domain.

Because sin and death entered the world (not just persons; Rom. 8:19–21), they qualified the human situation long before the law of Moses appeared on the scene. Although it was "added because of transgressions" (Gal. 3:19), it could not "make alive"—lead to life-giving rightness before God (Gal. 3:21). The reason is now clear: the law is heard only by persons in the domain of sin, under the tyranny of sin and death. In this situation, the actual function of the law with respect to God is to make everyone "accountable to God" and, with respect to the self, to produce "knowledge of sin" (Rom. 3:20).

It must not be forgotten that Paul looked back on his pre-Christian life as one which, measured by law, was "blameless" (Phil. 3:6). This means that Paul does not say that the awareness of non-doing, of failure and of guilt, dog a person. Rather, awareness that "through the law comes knowledge of sin" is retrospective Christian insight into life under law. One of the illusions of life under law is that one can succeed, especially more than others (as Rom. 2:17–24 makes clear).

Students of Paul, not only Jews, sometimes complain that Paul has misrepresented what Torah meant in Judaism. This is correct —and beside the point, for Paul does not intend to present the Jewish view of the law but his Christian perception of it. Only from the standpoint of life in Christ, in the Spirit, in the new age, in trust/faith, does the law look like this.

The foregoing observation is crucial for interpreting Rom. 7: 7–25. The whole discussion is designed to make it clear that it is not the law that causes sin, that the law and sin are not equatable (Rom. 7:7); rather, "the law is holy, and the commandment is holy and just and good" (v. 12). The ensuing discussion, however, contains several stubborn problems which vex interpreters. (a) At v. 7 Paul begins writing "I." How is this "I" to be understood— as a stylistic "I" or autobiographically? (b) What is the significance of the change to present tense in v. 14? The two problems are intertwined. On the one hand, if Paul writes autobiographically, and if the tense-shift is to be taken at face value, then he recounts his personal history with the law, up to the present. On the other hand, if the "I" is stylistic, then the subject may be the Adamic self, and the shift to the present tense may also be stylistic—a matter of rhetorical vividness. The crucial issue is whether vv. 14–25 have in view Christian experience or pre-Christian. Augustine, Luther, Calvin, and some more recent commentators have insisted that Paul is probing Christian existence, including his own; other recent exegetes insist that the "I am sold under sin" (v. 14) cannot refer to the status of the Christian, especially in view of Rom. 6:14 and 8:2. Either way, Paul reasons as a Christian; he does not portray the Jew's self-awareness.

Even if these paragraphs do describe *our* Christian experience with the law, the exegetical question is whether that is what *Paul* was saying. (a) Paul begins by exposing how the law functions with reference to sin: the law provoked sin into action, so that "I died" (v. 9). (Since it is difficult to regard "I was once alive apart from the law" as referring to any point in Paul's own life, there is merit in the suggestion that here "I" refers to Adam.) It is sin that perverts the situation so that "the very commandment which promised life proved to be death to me." The real character of sin is disclosed by the way it works through the good (the law). (b) Beginning with v. 15, Paul explains the contradiction between what one wills and what one actually does. Again, the point is that "if I do what I do not want [i.e., what is contrary to the law] I agree that the law is good." But then, who is the real doer? Not "I" but this other reality in me, sin. "I am sold under sin." The good does not reside in me, but sin does. (V. 18 has been mistranslated for centuries as "nothing good dwells in me"; it must be rendered "the good does not dwell in me." Paul is not answering the question, How much good dwells in me? but rather, Does the good dwell within me at all?) (c) So persistent is this disparity between intent and result that "I find it to be law that when I want to do right, evil lies close at hand." In fact, the inner self delights in God's law but yet it is at war with "another law" which resides in one's "members" (organs of the body) because the empirical self (*sōma*, body) is the means through which death and sin exercise influence.

In other words, because the good does not reside in the self, one cannot simply actualize oneself, bring out an inherent goodness—it is not there. The good has rather to be achieved. Yet this cannot be done for the will is vitiated by the power of sin and death. Paul does not blame physicality any more than he blames the law; he insists instead that the problem is sin which perverts everything, including the law (Rom. 8:3). Because sin and death reign over the self that hears the law (even if sin is not activated until one encounters obligation, it is still there), one cannot gain true life (rectitude before God) by doing what the law asks. Hearing the law only makes matters worse. There is only one solution—being set free from this bondage by being transferred to a domain where the Spirit prevails and where Christ is Lord; there the "just requirement of the law" (Rom. 8:4) can be fulfilled precisely because one is "not under the law but under grace" (Rom. 6:14).

Whether Paul unpacks pre-Christian or Christian experience with the law, the analysis itself is grounded in the resolution of the dilemma. Moreover, as Käsemann's commentary points out, Romans 7 stands as a warning against concluding that the Christian can fare any better with the law as a way of life than the non-Christian. The Christian can do "the just requirement of the law" only by ceasing to live "under the law." Precisely the devout, religious affirmer of the law of God is exposed as being condemned to inevitable failure. Just as the failure of capitalism becomes apparent only to one who ceases to live by it (e.g., a Marxist), and just as the failure of communism becomes apparent to one who abandons it, so the failure of law is evident only to one who is no longer "under the law but under grace." The greatest illusion of all is the idea that those in Christ can play the achiever's game successfully because they are Christians.

THE GOD WHO KEEPS FAITH

The moral integrity of God manifests itself also with regard to the future, the "not yet." Like Abraham, the Christian is fully convinced that God can keep his word (Rom. 4:21). The trustworthiness of God with respect to the completion of what is inaugurated in Christ was axiomatic for Paul; it underlies this view of the two ages (see p. 77), the gift of the Spirit as down-payment and first-fruits (see p. 102), the present reign of Christ (see p. 47), and the hope of Christ's imminent coming. What Paul wrote to the Philippians runs through his entire theological stance: "I am sure that he who began a good work in you will bring it to completion at the day of Jesus Christ" (Phil. 1:6). Paul insists, "God is faithful" (1 Cor. 1:9; 10:13; 2 Cor. 1:18; 1 Thess. 5:24).

Because God keeps faith in accord with the Christ-event, Paul can appropriate the dialectic of the cross/resurrection for his own life and work. To begin with, in the face of the coming Judgment (1 Cor. 4:12–15; 2 Cor. 5:10; 1 Thess. 5:9–11), Paul has remarkable confidence, for he is already rectified, his relation to God is already right. Since God has invested so much in the work of rectification, he will not cop out now (Rom. 8:31–34). So the coming Judgment is not something to be dreaded, but to be looked forward to as an event of vindication (1 Cor. 1:7–9; 15:58; Phil. 1:27–28; 1 Thess. 5:9–11). Paul expects also his mission to be vindicated, and he expressed a certain pride in his congregations insofar as they live by the gospel (Rom. 15:17–21; 2 Cor. 1:13–14; 3:1–3; Phil. 2:14–16; 1 Thess. 2:19–20).

Second, because it is God who will judge (or Christ, see p. 47), Paul is free from the compulsion of seeking approbation now (1 Cor. 4:1–7; 2 Cor. 10:18; 1 Thess. 2:3–6). He urges the same for his readers (Rom. 12:19–21; 14:10–13).

Third, confidence in God also gives Paul a critical distance from himself and his hard experiences. It really does not matter whether he lives or dies, for he belongs to the Lord in any case (Rom. 14: 8–9). Paul learned to live with difficulties and successes (Phil. 4:11–13). In fact, lest his hearers concluded that the gospel is powerful when and because he is impressive, Paul deliberately did not shirk appearing to be "weak" so that the Corinthians' response might be directed all the more clearly to God (1 Cor. 2:2–5). He rejected the possibility of proclaiming himself (2 Cor. 4:1–6). The dialectic of the cross/resurrection is the hallmark of authentic ministers of the gospel, who are clay pots for the real treasure (2 Cor. 4:7). So Paul points out that "we are afflicted in every way, but not crushed . . . always carrying in the body the death of Jesus, so that the life of Jesus [resurrection life] may also be manifested in our bodies" (2 Cor. 4:7–12). He does not have to appear as a winner all the time.

Paul emphasizes this point because the "false apostles" who

derailed the Corinthians apparently presented themselves as strong (whereas Paul was weak; 2 Cor. 10:10), eloquent (whereas Paul was not an impressive speaker; 2 Cor. 11:6), claiming that they were worthy to be supported financially (whereas Paul took no money from current converts; 2 Cor. 12:13–16). So Paul wrote with sharp irony of *his* manifest achievements: five times 39 lashes, three times beaten with rods, once stoned, all sorts of dangers and deprivations—all of which manifest his weakness (2 Cor. 11:21–12:10). The God who "chose what is weak in the world to shame the strong" (1 Cor. 2:27), who acted salvifically through the weak and vulnerable Jesus answered Paul's prayer for deliverance from a physical affliction, "My grace is sufficient for you, for my power is made perfect in weakness" (2 Cor. 12:7–9). Difficult experiences, which Paul regarded as a way of sharing Christ's sufferings (2 Cor. 1:5; Phil. 3:10–11) taught him to "rely not on ourselves but on God who raises the dead" (2 Cor. 1:9).

A person can write this way only if Jesus' cross/resurrection is the criterion of what God really is. Such a God is faithful also to Paul in precisely the same way as he was to Jesus—i.e., he who did not spare his Son (Rom. 8:32) will not spare Paul sufferings, vulnerability, weakness, or distress either. Yet nothing can separate Paul—or anyone else who trusts this God—from God's love in Christ, not even death.

The gospel for which Paul fought so strenuously and passionately is centered in the God who liberated humanity from bondage to sin, death, and law by sending his Son to be born under the law (Gal. 4:4), to be identified with sin (2 Cor. 5:21) and subject to death (Rom. 6:9). For those who believe this, the Christ-event strips away illusions about who God is and who they are.

We have sought to follow Paul's theological pointers to see whether what he saw can be seen again. He did not see everything; indeed, he himself insisted that he saw but dimly and knew but partly (1 Cor. 13:12). But he fought for the integrity of what he knew, confident that "we can do nothing against the truth, but only for the truth" (2 Cor. 13:8).

SELECTED BIBLIOGRAPHY

(Includes all works mentioned in the text)

BARRETT, C. K., *The First Epistle to the Corinthians* (New York: Harper and Row, 1968).

BORNKAMM, G., *Paul* (New York: Harper and Row, 1971).

BULTMANN, R., *Existence and Faith,* S. Ogden, ed. (Cleveland: World, Meridian Books, 1960).

BULTMANN, R., *Theology of the New Testament,* 1 and 2 (New York: Scribner's, 1954, 1955).

CULLMANN, O., *Christ and Time* (Philadelphia: Westminster Press, 1950).

DAHL, N., *Studies in Paul* (Minneapolis: Augsburg, 1977).

DEISSMANN, A., *Paul* (New York: Harper & Row [Torchbook ed.], 1957 [orig. ed. 1912]).

DOTY, W., *Letters in Primitive Christianity* (Philadelphia: Fortress Press, 1973).

DONFRIED, K., *The Romans Debate* (Minneapolis: Augsburg, 1977).

DUNGAN, D., *The Sayings of Jesus in the Churches of Paul* (Philadelphia: Fortress Press, 1971).

FARMER, W., MOULE, C., NIEBUHR, R. eds., *Christian History and Interpretation* (Cambridge: Cambridge University Press, 1967).

FURNISH, V., *Theology and Ethics in Paul* (Nashville: Abingdon Press, 1968).

KÄSEMANN, E., *New Testament Questions of Today* (Philadelphia: Fortress Press, 1969).

KÄSEMANN, E., *Perspectives on Paul* (Philadelphia: Fortress Press, 1971).

131

KECK, L. and MARTYN, J. L., eds., *Studies in Luke–Acts* (Nashville: Abingdon Press, 1966).

MARTIN, R., *Carmen Christi* (Cambridge: Cambridge University Press, 1967).

MUNCK, J., *Paul and the Salvation of Mankind* (Atlanta: John Knox Press, 1977 [orig. ed. 1959]).

PAGELS, E., *The Gnostic Paul* (Philadelphia: Fortress Press, 1975).

RICHARDSON, A., "Salvation," *Interpreter's Dictionary of the Bible* 4, pp. 168–181.

RIDDERBOS, H., *Paul* (Grand Rapids: Eerdmans, 1975).

SANDERS, E. P., *Paul and Palestinian Judaism* (Philadelphia: Fortress Press, 1977).

SCHMITHALS, W., *Gnosticism in Corinth* (Nashville: Abingdon Press, 1971 [orig. ed. 1956]).

SCHMITHALS, W., *Paul and the Gnostics* (Nashville: Abingdon Press, 1972).

SCROGGS, R., *The Last Adam* (Philadelphia: Fortress Press, 1966).

SCROGGS, R., *Paul for a New Day* (Philadelphia: Fortress Press, 1977).

STENDAHL, K., *Paul Among Jews and Gentiles* (Philadelphia: Fortress Press, 1976).

TANNEHILL, R., *Dying and Rising with Christ* (Berlin: Töpelmann, 1966).

INDEX